UNIVERSITIES IN THE TWENTY-FIRST
A Lecture Series

UNIVERSITIES IN THE TWENTY-FIRST CENTURY
A Lecture Series

Universities in the Twenty-first Century

A Lecture Series

Paul Hamlyn Foundation
NATIONAL COMMISSION
ON EDUCATION
AND
The Council for Industry and Higher Education

The National Commission on Education
Director: Sir John Cassels CB

The Commission was established in 1991 by the British Association for the Advancement of Science with the support of the Royal Society, the British Academy, and the Fellowship of Engineering (now the Royal Academy of Engineering). Its purpose has been to identify and examine key issues facing education and training in the United Kingdom in the next twenty-five years. Its report *Learning to Succeed: A Radical Look at Education Today and a Strategy for the Future* was published in November 1993.

The Commission is an independent body funded by the Paul Hamlyn Foundation. It is not associated in any way with any political party.

The Council for Industry and Higher Education
Director: Patrick Coldstream CBE

The Council for Industry and Higher Education is an entirely independent body financed by company contributions and made up of heads of companies, vice chancellors and heads of other higher education institutions. Its purpose is to encourage industry and higher education to mark out common interests, to work together, and to represent their joint thinking to government, universities and companies.

Copyright © National Commission on Education and Council for Industry and Higher Education 1994

The text may be reproduced and quoted without permission provided that its source is acknowledged

First Published March 1994

ISBN 0-9523114-0-2

All enquiries should be directed to:
The National Commission on Education
Suite 24, 10–18 Manor Gardens
London N7 6JY

Published by the National Commision on Education
Printed and bound in Great Britain by Latimer Trend & Company Ltd

Contents

Foreword

I am pleased that BT has been able to assist the publication of this excellent book. As a company we work closely with higher education in a number of ways and acknowledge the vital role that the sector plays in supporting the commercial well-being of the country. I applaud the decision of the National Commission on Education and the Council for Industry and Higher Education to publish these lectures which challenge assumptions about higher education and create a practical vision for the future.

Sir Iain Vallance
Chairman British Telecommunications plc

Preface

This series of lectures, *Universities in the Twenty-first Century*, was arranged jointly by the National Commission on Education and the Council for Industry and Higher Education against a background of expansion and change in British higher education. The last of the six lectures, which were delivered in the spring of 1993, was given on 31 March, the very day upon which the national binary system was dismantled. On that day, the Polytechnics and Colleges and Funding Council (PCFC) and the Universities Funding Council (UFC) were dissolved and, the following day, responsibility for the funding of a new regionalised unitary sector was assumed by the Higher Education Funding Council for England (HEFCE), and its counterparts in Scotland, Wales and Northern Ireland. In May 1991, in *Higher Education: A New Framework*, the Government had stated 'It can be expected that nearly one in three of all young people will enter higher education by the year 2000, and that participation by mature entrants will also increase'. By the time these lectures were being given, it was clear that the Government's target would be achieved well before the end of the century, and that mature people taking advantage of opportunities in higher education were already making up more than half of the student population.

Changes of this significance and rapidity in a sector which has hitherto been relatively selective and homogeneous are presenting an enormous challenge to those who are responsible for its leadership and management, and for maintaining the standards of high quality education for which the British system rightly receives international recognition. The seriousness of the issues to be tackled becomes ever more evident as the impact of recession and continued financial constraint highlight the need to give value for money in all aspects of provision. And, all the indications are that the pace of change in higher education will accelerate, as institutions seek to meet the needs of their growing and increasingly diverse customer base. As we move into the next century the challenges will grow rather than diminish.

Considerations of this nature led the Commission and the Council to mount this lecture series with the aim of bringing together a wide range of people with a stake in the future of higher education and training – academics, industrialists, policy-makers, students, and those involved in the management both of the higher education system and of individual institutions – to promote joint discussion of how higher education can best meet the future economic and social needs of the United Kingdom, and to develop a vision for the longer term role of the universities.

In planning the series, we were concerned to explore the future for higher education from a range of different perspectives. We wanted not only to take the views of those within the system and involved in crucial aspects of its funding, but also to hear from the business community and learn from the experience of other countries. We also hoped that the series would influence the thinking within the National Commission on the developing roles and interface between further and higher education. We were fortunate, in the event, to secure an outstanding group of lecturers, who more than exceeded our expectations and, collectively, built up a vision of the future which inspired us with its optimism, while never departing from the hard, practical considerations implicit in its achievement. Some of the issues raised have, indeed, already been taken further in the National Commission's report, *Learning to Succeed: A Radical Look at Education Today and a Strategy for the Future*, which was published in November 1993.

The Commission and the Council are enormously grateful to the lecturers for the very different but wholly stimulating lectures, and for agreeing to their subsequent publication, in edited form, in this volume. I am also particularly grateful to Patrick Coldstream and Sir John Cassels for their part in the inception, planning and execution of the series.

As series Chairman, I was assisted in my task by Baroness Perry of Southwark, Vice-Chancellor and Chief Executive of South Bank University, Dr Alan Rudge, Managing Director, Development and Procurement, BT plc, Helena Kennedy QC, Chair of the National Commission on Education's Working Group on Further and Higher

Education, and Lord Walton of Detchant, Chairman of the National Commission on Education, and I should like to thank each one of them for their informed comment and skilful direction of the discussions which followed each lecture and are published in edited version in this volume.

The lectures took place at the Royal Society, and I should like to thank the Society and its staff for their help and support. Special thanks also go to Helen Kinnings, who organised the series with considerable efficiency, and to Gwynneth Rigby for editing this volume.

Finally I should like to thank BT plc, who generously sponsored the publication of this volume, and made its dissemination possible.

John Raisman CBE
Series Chairman

Chairman of the Council for Industry and Higher Education and Deputy Chairman of the National Commission on Education January 1994

1
The Idea of a University?
Professor Stewart Sutherland, Vice-Chancellor,
University of London

Prologue

These lectures have created an opportunity – which, as a philosopher by discipline, I greatly welcome – to give some careful thought
to what we mean by the word 'university' and what defining characteristics, if any, can be attributed to it. But, as a prologue, let me
stress that the horizon must be the twenty-first century. One of the
major problems besetting universities in the United Kingdom for
the last two decades has been a preoccupation with the short term.
This has meant, at best, a tension between short-term and long-term
priorities, and at worst a neglect of the long-term.

I can illustrate this with reference to the question of size of institutions and student numbers. For some, the ideal seems to have been
– or indeed still is – small interactive institutions, built on the model
of collegiality. There has undoubtedly been pressure from outside
the system to expand – although it has to be said that the message
has suddenly been muted. Upon reflection, this is nothing new.
Indeed, the recent Christmas pantomime season led me to recall the
dialogue over the last thirty years being something like this:

1960s and 1970s:

Government:	You will expand!
Universities:	Oh no we won't!
Government:	Oh yes you will, or we shall give all the money to the colleges of advanced technology (CATs) and the new universities!
Universities:	Oh yes we will!

1

1981 to 1988

Government:	You will stop expanding!
Universities:	Oh no we won't!
Government:	Oh yes you will, or we shall fine you for each student over quota whom you admit!
Universities:	Oh yes we will!

1988 to 1992

Government:	You will expand!
Universities:	Oh no we won't!
Government:	Oh yes you will, or we shall give all the extra money to the polytechnics!
Universities:	Oh yes we will!

1992-

Government:	You will stop expanding!
Universities:	Oh no we probably won't
Government:	Oh yes you will, or ...

At this point I wakened from my nightmare and decided that I preferred the more rational world of pantomime! The serious point is that the question of the size of the system, and of the size of individual institutions within it – which has had to preoccupy some of us just a little too much because of the fairly abrupt swings in Government policy – is a secondary question. It is not a defining question. Universities can be of many and varied sizes. Equally, however, it is a fundamental error to create a system that equates expansion – or for that matter contraction – with success. Some institutions will be the better remaining the size that they are for the foreseeable future.

The first lesson that I draw is, therefore, that the question of size is secondary and is subject to two other concepts, to which I shall return shortly; that is, education and standards.

An Evolutionary Process

The reference in the title of this lecture is to John Henry Newman's remarkable meditation, *The Idea of a University*, composed in the early 1850s without any thought of the question-mark which I have attached to it. Let me illustrate the force of the question-mark in two ways. The first is to give a subtitle to the lecture: 'The Idea is dead, long live the Universities'. The second is to declare an interest, possibly a prejudice, and certainly a grievance. It is reported that when Henry Brougham and his colleagues were engaging public interest in the proposal to found a university in London Newman showed all the prejudice which might have been expected in 1826 of a young fellow of Oriel, and referred to the proposed creation as a 'bazaar' or a 'pantechnicon'.

I tell the story, not simply to give some reassurance to the 'new' universities that little changes beneath certain skins in academe, nor simply to say 'join the club', but rather to make a fairly fundamental point – there is no single criterion, necessary and sufficient, of what counts as a university. It is not, however, my intention to use this lecture to give a scholarly critique and exposition of Newman's book. Suffice it to say that I am claiming that his case is fundamentally flawed in its implicit assumption that we can give a single clear account of what constitutes the *idea* of a university.

That, however, is the easy part. For, when Newman asked himself what a university was, he was asking a reasonable question which has not been rendered anachronistic by the very variety about which he had clear misgivings. Nevertheless, just as the Edinburgh of his day was different from Jowett's Oxford, the difficulty which he would have in recognising M.I.T., or Imperial College, or University College, London, as fitting his *idea*, would probably be just as pronounced if he were to turn his gaze on the variety which is present-day Oxford. But the root-puzzlement of his question still stands for, even in such distinguished variety, we have no difficulty in recognising each of them as universities. And yet, in virtue of what do we make this confident assertion? For, with equal confidence, we are able to pick out all sorts of institutions which are not universities. For example, whatever common concerns and values they share, neither Manchester Grammar School, nor Roedean, nor Woodside Primary School are universities; nor is the Dupont Research Park, nor the Arsenal Football Club, nor the Sun Newspaper. Again, in each case, we have no difficulty in coming to clear and prompt answers.

The point, or indeed the dilemma, is this: we seem to be able to recognise examples of universities, despite the absence of a single clear definition of what a university is, let alone a set of necessary and sufficient criteria.

As the storyteller of old used to say when in a spot: 'let me digress'. The subject of my digression is the concept – or idea – of number. There are some parallels; we can recognise examples of numbers – even the least numerate amongst us knows that 2, 22, 105, 17, and 3,000,046, are all numbers. Indeed, we know it without necessarily having clear in our respective minds what the definition of number is. The interesting point, however, about the definition of number is that it has evolved. What counts as a number has changed, and indeed expanded. This expansion took place alongside, and was a condition of, the development of mathematics. And you do not have to have a PhD in maths to appreciate the point. As the Greeks and others who followed them developed and extended mathematics, they developed the range and definition of the idea of what could count as a number. So, to whole positive numbers such as 2, 22, and so on, was added the idea of non-whole numbers, fractions such as $1/2$ or $3/4$. The idea of negative numbers, such as -5 or -183 was also added. Each of these extensions to the idea was an extension of the capacity of arithmetic in both theoretical and practical contexts.

The point of my digression is that important ideas expand and develop, and are not constrained wholly by the first examples of the class. There may well have been those in the early academies who wrote to the *Athens Times*, or the *Spartan Telegraph*, lamenting the diminution in numerical purity resulting from the admission to the arithmetical Athenaeum of such upstarts as negative numbers and fractions. But, one has to ask, where they are now?

Acknowledging this, however, is a far cry from suggesting that all change is inevitably change for the better. There was a logic to the extension of the class of what counted as a number. There were reasons, largely the internal reasons of mathematics, for enlarging the 'club' in this way. There are equally cogent examples of the extension of the meanings of words in ways which have diminished their usefulness to the point of emptying them of almost all meaning. For example, the words 'sentiment' and 'sentimental' had positive and robust qualities implied in their use in the eighteenth century which have now been lost. The words 'emotion' and 'emotional' have virtually suffered the same fate in this century. The consistent overuse of words such as 'rights' and 'democratic' in the last thirty years is an even more important cause for concern. What then about the word 'university'?

Firstly, there has been significant diversity for some considerable time. In Scotland, in the nineteen-fifties this was tacitly acknowledged by using the word 'university' to refer to all the examples then existing, but with primary association with good solid robust institutions like Aberdeen, Edinburgh, Glasgow and St Andrews. A truncation of it – varsity – was used to refer to two rather more effete specimens in the south! In any case the diversity was recognised.

Secondly, the range of subjects taught in universities has enlarged in very significant ways. For example, it was thought very daring for a relatively new institution, University College, London, to found a chair in engineering, or for the University, later in the nineteenth century, to pioneer the introduction of english literature as a subject of study. And of course the extension of the curriculum in the last hundred years or so has been dramatic: biochemistry, followed by microbiology, genetics and biotechnology; accountancy, business studies, management studies; social work, nursing studies, and physiotherapy. It is very easy to think of a period, in the not-too-distant past, when the very idea of any of the subjects mentioned in this paragraph being legitimate subjects of a university degree courses would have been quite unacceptable.

There is also a point of reverse snobbery. It is sometimes implied that the idea of vocational courses is a new invention – something that traditional universities did not do, but that new or aspirant universities were bringing to the debate. At each extreme of the profession there was collusion in sustaining this myth, as both the intellectual luddites and the rude mechanicals conveniently forgot that the older universities had been in the business of training lawyers, doctors and clergymen for centuries. Fortunately, most members of the profession whether from old, young or middle-aged universities, were quite well aware of the truth of the matter and, as academics usually do, got on with the business in hand of developing their own research and teaching, whether in the context of vocational education or not.

Two Fundamental Questions

Anything Goes?

So much then for the importance of flexibility and extendability in our idea of a university. 'But', Disgusted of Brideshead cries, 'where will it all end? Is there no limit to what can pass for legitimate activity in a university? Shall we soon have masters courses in Advanced Hairdressing? Or perhaps the London cab drivers will vote to become a graduate-entry profession, with reduced probationary periods for those with a combined honours B.A. in Contemporary Society and *The Knowledge*?' Of course, it is not the case that 'anything goes', but it was more difficult than I had first imagined to construct examples which, at least at first blush, were unlikely to be contentious.

As we noted from the example of the extension of the range and definition of the word 'number', there was a reference to an inner logic at work, so that reasons acceptable to mathematicians, and through them to the canons of mathematical though, could be given to justify the presence of the new members of the Numbers Club. In noting this, we have, I believe, arrived at the central issue which confronts the developing university system in the United Kingdom.

Who Decides?

I have argued that the extension of the concept of number took place within the context of rules recognised by mathematicians. The key to the inner logic of the concept, in the end, was held by them. What about the extension and changes in the idea of a university? I have in mind here, not so much the changes which have taken place – although each of these would bear interesting historical scrutiny – but the changes which will take place, changes which perhaps few if any of us can envisage at the moment. If there are to be limits to such change – and, for the reasons given, surely there must be – who will, at any one time, set those limits? What is the logic governing such change? Who are the final arbiters in case of dispute?

The issue here is not one of legality, for that is quite clearly settled in this country. The status of a university is attached to the power to award degrees, and that is granted either by Charter, or by Act of Parliament. Also, it is clearly the case, by implication, that what any degree-awarding body deems to be a degree-level subject for study has that status within that institution. Rather the issue concerns the canons by which such institutions make decisions about their future profile and portfolio of activities. It also concerns the constraints under which such judgements are formulated, and such decisions taken.

In considering the location of decision-making, it is regarded as very significant by many academics that there is consistent pressure either from Government or from Vice-Chancellors to introduce new and alien styles of management into what has been essentially a collegiate system. There is some evidence for this, not least in the ways in which our language has changed: 'departments' have become 'cost-centres', 'students' have become 'full-time equivalents (FTEs for short)' and so on. However, this is not as new as some believe. For a long time now, heads of large science departments or research groups have had major managerial roles with regard to budget and the deployment of all grades of staff. The managerial style of an institution must reflect the responsibilities of its decision-makers, and their need to formulate and achieve objectives. What is critical, however, is that questions which are genuinely academic questions should be dealt with by academics – for example, questions about academic standards, about the academic acceptability of courses, and about the quality of research output.

This, then is the second lesson. Questions of academic standards, and of the acceptability of goals as legitimate academic goals are for academic decision. Management is a matter of matching resources to goals, of matching both against achievement, and of ensuring that other institutional goals are compatible with basic academic objectives.

Conclusions

It is now time to try to point to some more general conclusions, but I have made the task more difficult for myself than it might be by drawing a less precise picture of the content of the idea of a university than Newman's original phrase seemed to promise. I have stressed that the concept, like the institutions to which it collectively refers, is in a process of evolution. Had those who started in the business a quarter of a century or more ago been shown the current menu of activities which constitute university education, we should have had reactions lying somewhere between surprise and amazement. *Mutatis mutandis,* doubtless the same will apply to those who survive the next quarter of a century or so with sufficient curiosity to look back to 1993.

In such flux our questions, 'does anything go?' and 'who decides?' become increasingly central to dealing with the question-mark which I have put after Newman's title. This much I share with Newman, that there are certain basic concepts, which must determine all other judgements which we make about what counts as university activity – that is to say, which give us the capacity to say, 'No, it is not the case that anything goes'. I shall further argue that ultimately, because of the nature of those concepts, the judgements in question must ultimately be made by academics. Hence my answer to the first question is that it is not the case that anything goes, and to the second question is that the decisions must be made by the community of academics. Let me expand on why this should be so.

The comparison with the example of the extension of the concept of number will be helpful. Just as any expansion of the range of what counts as a number is connected to and compatible with the enterprise of mathematics and the logic – the pattern of reasoning – specific to that discipline, as well as the dominant ideas which already have a life within that discipline – such as addition, subtraction, division and so on – so, in the extension of the concept of a university to include much that is new there must, nonetheless, be a similar set of points of reference. This alone would allow us to determine whether the extension of the idea is, in fact, an extension of a living tradition, or whether it is a departure so radical that we are talking about the birth of something quite new.

Fortunately there are such basic concepts to hand and I shall briefly discuss three of them: education, research, and standards.

Education
The first important point to be made is that education may include training and the imparting of skills. But it is much more than that. One can train a rat to respond to a bell or some other stimulus: one might even talk of the rat learning. One can even train someone of my generation to work the video-recorder, and again one might talk of it as a triumph of middle-aged learning. But in neither case

would such training or acquisition of skills be properly classified as education. Why not? Because although it may impart skills and the ability to respond, it does not give understanding.

Understanding as a defining criterion of the goal of education differentiates education from training in a number of ways. Specifically, someone who understands a technique or a concept is not bound by the specific form in which that skill was first acquired. Understanding brings with it the capacity to modify one's skills to deal with similar but significantly different problems; to apply one's reasoning abilities to new problems; to grasp why this adaption is appropriate, and that inappropriate. In a particular field of study, be it chemistry or history, understanding implies the ability to recognise faulty reasoning, to construct hypotheses which go beyond the evidence available and to identify the kinds of evidence which will verify or falsify the hypothesis. Training and the imparting of skills, can legitimately fall well short of that.

With something like that distinction in mind, we can see how we can be guided to give answers to whole series of questions of both primary and secondary status. Thus the question of which fields of study are appropriate for a university to promote is in part a question of which fields of human knowledge or ability are most properly dealt with via education rather than simply training. I argue that, in this context, higher education has two characteristics. First, it involves the development of a pattern of understanding which is fundamentally cumulative and hierarchical in nature. Second – and this is closely related – the proposed field of study must have a theoretical underpinning which can in principle be probed, extended and tested. Understanding is the capacity to engage in that process of probing, testing, and extending.

Research
My contention here is not that everyone in a university should inevitably be engaged in research, nor certainly that the sole point of education is to produce researchers. Rather, for the reasons given above about the theoretical foundations of admissible fields of study, any subject which is genuinely a university subject will be one which is capable of further development. The corollary of that is, that if all that there is to be known in this field is already in principle known, then it is not an appropriate subject for a university degree,

although it may contribute, as a building block, to another degree programme which does pass this particular test.

It is here, I believe, that we shall find the genuine logic for locating teaching and research in the same institution. The argument is not that inevitably every good teacher must be a researcher. It is more subtle than that. It is rather that the fields of study appropriate for university degree work are such that, in principle, they extend to boundaries which are not their final resting place – or, more dramatically, that from the first undergraduate introduction to them they extend, so to speak, to infinity, or to that particular frontier of human knowledge. If education is to be offered, and understanding is to be the outcome, then a crucial element of that understanding must be that our knowledge is not complete, that further extension beyond the current limits of our grasp of the subject is both possible and required. To grasp that is to be aware of what research in that subject could mean. To educate in that subject is to be aware of what the current limits are and, in principle, where the points of development might be.

Thus chemistry and history, for example, are appropriate fields of study because, in the first place, there are theories and methods which show us how to extend our knowledge and understanding, how to gain new insights, how to test the strength of those insights. Equally the theories and methods which we use to build our understanding are themselves, in principle, subject to revision. That is to say, knowledge and understanding in these fields are always to some extent provisional.

Further, education in these fields will be, in part, aimed at ensuring that the students understand that there is this degree of provisionality – that we are not concerned with learning a complete and completed set of dogmas about which no further questions can arise. This applies as much to theology and politics as it does to chemistry and history. It also shows why there is a natural and inevitable link between research and the extension of knowledge and education as it is practised in universities. This has nothing to do with whether researchers are the best or worst teachers and sterile arguments of that sort, but rather with the subject-matter appropriate to the university system. These fields of study lead naturally and inevitably to boundary situations, and understanding – which is the product of education at that level – requires a grasp, at least, of where the boundaries of knowledge are and what is being done to extend them.

Standards
This takes me easily to the third key concept which must inform us about the evolution of the system. The concept of standards is important in a variety of ways. The first is the formal responsibility which universities have, in this context, of setting the standards or output measures of what counts as degree-level work. We neglect this at our peril.

The second is that, as a consequence of what I have argued above, acquiring a degree will be a testing business intellectually and in other ways – it will be difficult. This has a number of consequences, not least that students will require the help of good teaching, and facilities which are adequate for developing the kind of understanding to which I have referred. Not only are outputs important, so also is process.

The third is that the extension of knowledge is not confined to local or parochial contexts. Knowledge, like understanding, should have an international horizon and, for this very clear reason, truth and falsehood are not constrained by local boundaries – they are 'panhuman' or international in character. High standards in research or the extension of knowledge are not the preserve of any one group, department, or nation. What counts as high quality research is, in the end, a matter for an international agenda.

Practical Questions

It follows from all that I have said that there will nonetheless be immense variety in the university system. If the centrality which they deserve is given to the three key concepts which I have outlined – education, research and standards – there will develop an approximate set of relations or – to be blunt – a hierarchy between institutions. This hierarchy can have one of two basic forms, as shown in Figures 1 and 2.

Model A simply accepts that there will be some universities that are research focused, and some that are teaching focused, and that there will be feeder colleges and institutions. Under this model there will be a very clear hierarchy. Each institution will know where it is in the pecking order, and will know very clearly what its objectives ought to be.

Figure 1: Model A

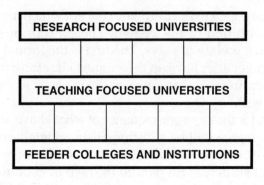

Model B is more complicated and nearer the present reality. This model accepts that in this country we do not have universities that are purely research-based, but that we do have some post-graduate institutions that are very important in the university system. Most institutions are research and teaching focused (R&T) and many others are teaching institutions with some research activity (T&R). There are some which are focused only on teaching (T) – a role which some colleges have already adopted very successfully. But alongside these there may well develop T-focused universities. Certainly, we are already seeing T-focused departments developing within some universities. Feeding into these various institutions will be a range of colleges and institutions.

Model B is not just a more complex model, but it is one which will continue to allow evolution. It is for this reason that I prefer it to the hierarchical and highly structured Model A which would make change and extension into new areas considerably more difficult.

If all that I say about education and understanding, about flexibility of mind, capacity to weigh evidence, to make judgements, and to enter imaginatively into situations not determined by one's own egocentric standpoint are more than high-flown words, then there is a basic question and a fairly clear acid-test which I commend to my fellow academics.

Figure 2: Model B

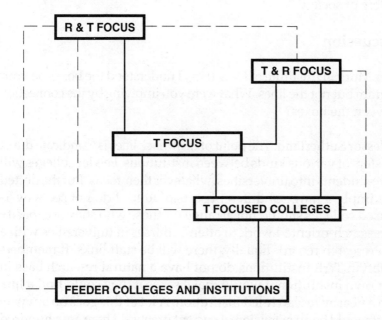

The question is: does university education produce an educated person? One hunch which I do share with Newman is that we must not let the idea of 'an educated person' languish unused. I am not thinking here of additional half course-units in citizenship or the like, nor am I thinking of a list of a hundred and one things which the well educated person needs to know – apart that is from the literacy and numeracy which we ought to be able to take for granted. The acid-test is then: suppose we suddenly discover that a recent graduate from our department or institution is (a)our local MP; (b)the local planning officer; (c)the magistrate on the bench now hearing our case. Are we (i)reassured, (ii)amazed or (iii)struck dumb with horror? If so, why?

This, then is my concluding lesson. Whatever their particular specialism of study, those who have received a university education worthy of the name should, as a result, be better equipped to play a wide variety of public roles than if they had not had that advantage. This is, perhaps, a more popular version of the thought to be found in Newman and in Jowett and his successors, that university education should, amongst other things, help provide some of the leaders of society.

Discussion

Peter Morgan (Institute of Directors): I understood the boxes on your diagram but not the lines. What were you implying by the connection between the boxes?

Professor Sutherland: The point of firm black lines is to indicate direct transfers of various kinds between institutions. Feeder colleges will move students into universities, whatever their focus. But the dotted lines imply a range of different sorts of links. I do not see why T-focused colleges should not arrange for those who show a capacity for research-oriented work to attend courses in universities with a high research record. Equally, there will be staff links. If members of staff in T&R institutions do not have a natural research base in their own institution it would make sense if they could find a link with a nearby research-led institution. A lot of this goes on anyway and it would be an extension of current practice. There are a hundred and one other things – services being provided from one to another, making use of specialist libraries and equipment, and so on. As the funding pattern changes, I think we will have to do this.

Leslie Wagner (University of North London): Both your models for the higher education system showed a clear hierarchy. Your flows were all up from teaching to research. You suggested that a good researcher in a T&R might do some research in an R&T institution. You did not talk about a good teacher in an R&T university going the other way. Clearly therefore we have a value system. Why do we have that value system?

Professor Sutherland: In fact the flow lines do not have arrows on them, and I would like to see them going in a variety of direction. I think the idea that every single honours degree is dominated by the standards appropriate for those who intend to move on to a masters or a PhD course is a weakness in our system. People should be able to peel out, say in the second year, and extend their academic range. This might mean moving institution for the third year. It is the same as somebody who is very good at chemistry wishing to work in the pharmaceutical industry on the management side. It might well be right for them to consider taking courses in economics, in management studies, in company law or to acquire another language. I would like to see division points made possible within the degree programme, which would then allow the kind of movement you suggest.

I think we have to accept, however, that most academics think in terms of hierarchy and, given the opportunity to put letters like PhD or DSc after their name, would regard it as a significant step forward. The reason is that they are all concerned with the extension of knowledge in their subjects. It is characteristic of a university subject that it is capable of extension, that it is theory-laden, and that the critique of theory is integral to it. It is this which leads staff to place high value on research. And that is, by and large, a respectable reason. But, universities have not always been good at rewarding good teachers through promotion or in other ways. Good teachers also extend our understanding of the subject by developing the ways in which it can be taught, and taught to different and varied groups. I would want to persuade colleagues that, for example, a chair in engineering education would be highly desirable. I am not sure we are getting engineering education right. We should give status to individuals who can think what engineering is; what kinds of courses we provide, how we provide them, and how we deliver them; and what form of engineering education is needed for the future. Recognising that quality in teaching and giving it very high status would not reverse the hierarchy, but it would show that strengths can be found elsewhere.

Professor Gareth Williams (Centre for Higher Education Studies, Institute of Education): I would like to suggest that there may be a case to be made for Model A if you drew a few more of your dotted lines on it. There is a danger if you have a flexible system – which sounds good – of everybody in the whole system wanting to be like the institutions and the departments that are perceived to have the highest prestige, and of concentrating, therefore, on pushing research at the expense of teaching. It seems to me to be at least arguable that if you want really good teaching you create institutions where teaching is, in effect, the be-all and end-all of the institution. I would like your reflections on that view.

Professor Sutherland: If colleges and universities are focused purely on teaching, then it is a bit like some of my worries about secondary schools without sixth forms. It means that the range of teachers in those institutions will be much more circumscribed than it would otherwise be. There are advantages in having a mixture of teachers, some of whom are teaching-focused in their proper self-directed aims and some of whom combine teaching with research. Otherwise, you would introduce tremendous rigidity into academic career paths, with movement possible only from teaching to research. It would be very difficult to move in the other direction. If you entered the profession at the age of 25 or 26, with a doctorate, you would remain in that context for 40 years. The reality is different. There are some high-flying researchers who will always be at the leading edge; there are some who come and go; and some who have fallow periods and are happy to spend a lot more time thinking about their teaching and developing it on the basis of their research. So I think there are practical draw-backs to following Model A.

In fact, we are not at that point and, practically speaking, it would require fairly draconian funding principles that would bring much damage and harm in their wake to move quickly to it. I am much more pragmatic. I want to see the system begin to shake down, and I think it will shake down not by institution but, more probably, by faculty or department. There are advantages in that process. The last thing we need is another set of bright ideas and rigid funding-driven principles forcing institutions to go one way or the other. We would waste the next six years arguing about it if that became the official public policy.

Ron Barnett (Centre for Higher Education Studies, Institute of Education): Most teaching academics would say they are in the business of developing critical skills and, in the middle of this century, we did develop a notion of universities as critical centres in society. It is arguable that we are in the danger of losing that strand in our concept of the university. If a necessary criterion for our understanding of universities is that they are in the business of teaching core skills, it raises the question of the relationship between universities and society. Are universities simply in the business of providing the knowledge and competence that modern society wants or is there a necessary tension between the two?

Professor Sutherland: I talked earlier about the capacity to analyse, to decide whether reasons were good reasons, whether there was faulty reasoning, whether judgements were well founded, whether the evidential base was strong. In that sense universities are developing critical skills in their students.

As far as universities being critical centres in society is concerned, there are two points. First, society will, by and large, pay for what it wants. Society does, quite rightly, look to universities to provide skilled people who can take on jobs as GPs and lawyers, and who can act as magistrates and members of planning committees in their spare time. By and large people will pay for that sort of thing. But we also need to persuade society that it is important that taxpayers are willing to put money up to extend human knowledge. It may be that the motives for doing this vary between academics and taxpayers. If you are a taxpayer you will want a fairly clear picture of what you are getting for your money. If you are an academic you will want to follow the argument wherever it leads because it is fascinating. We have managed to accommodate this tension in the past and we must in the future.

Second, I have a lot of sympathy and respect for Carl Popper's view that as you develop the kind of analytical, evidential, rational skills that you are calling critical skills, in the context, say, of being a good physicist or historian, it requires a peculiar personality not to take those skills into other areas of life and apply them in reading the newspapers, listening to politicians or looking at an advertisement. The implications of this for a democratic society are very important indeed. Alistair MacIntyre has written some very interesting pieces on this in his recent Gifford lectures, *Three Versions of Moral Inquiry*. He takes the line, with which I fully agree, that a university must be a place where there is a clash and an interface between different ideologies and different sets of basic assumptions. But the idea that society will pay to have someone to point out its faults is one you have got to be a bit careful about. I think society is not inclined to do so, if you put it in those terms.

Professor R C D Aitken (Vice-Principal, University of Edinburgh): Could you give those of us who are involved in university management some advice on how to move our vision from a pre-occupation with the short term, where the ground seems to be constantly shifting, to long-term issues?

Professor Sutherland: I'm not all that enthusiastic about giving advice. What I like to do is have a good discussion about how to take a decision on a particular issue. But you do need clear lines of division about how you manage budgets, how you ensure that the right numbers of staff and the right equipment are in place, and how you provide adequate library facilities for your researchers and your students. All these employ very important skills that are not usually part of the training of academics, though more and more they are becoming so. You have got to find a balance within the institution between developing those skills in staff and encouraging their application, and enabling staff to stand back and, at critical points, identify issues of principle. Do we go down the road of accepting the first 'Minicab chair in *The Knowledge*' because not only are there funds for the chair but also for a new sports centre and a multi-storey car park provided, of course, that the sponsor gets the ground floor! Issues of principle must be raised, and those in management must be willing to sit down and thrash through with their fellow academics whether or not a given proposal is compatible with the objectives of the institution. Equally academics must be prepared to accept that hard decisions have to be taken and that, for example, cost-benefit analysis has a valid role to play in deciding between two equally good options. That is almost 'motherhood and apple pie' – and academics have become much more realistic over the last ten years – but I don't think we should let go of it, for all that.

Marianne Houghton (Student, Open University): I was struck by your remarks on the role of academics in management and decision-making. But how might students inform debate, if not actually take part in the decision-making that informs management?

Professor Sutherland: First, I think most sensible universities already have provision for student members of governing bodies and senates and my experience of that has been very positive indeed. I think it is important that they are part of the constitutional structure. Again any worthwhile university and department has mechanisms in place for sampling student opinion on detailed matters, like the courses that are available to them or whether or not the reading list is sensible, and the books on the reading list in the library – very practical matters. It provides a way for students, on behalf of others, to make points to their teachers without there being a personal confrontation. That is very important.

Secondly, what I would like to do is to get together groups of graduates, say five years on, to ask them to look back and to say what it was really like and, from their present perspective, to analyse the strengths and weaknesses and suggest what might need to be changed. That is actually quite difficult, since most graduate associations seem to be dominated by people who are fairly mature in years, whereas those who came through the system fairly recently and are most likely to contribute that kind of advice tend not to be very active.

Dick Coldwell (National Grid Company and Chairman of the Board, University of North London): Given current plans for expansion, and taking into account the kind of education and critical training you have described, is there a natural limit, in your mind, to the numbers of people you can put through the system?

Professor Sutherland: To be honest I don't think we know. Not very long ago, we would have expressed considerable surprise at a participation rate of 15%, and incredulity at a rate of 25%. But here we are, pushing over 25% to 30%. I think the right way to set the limit is to ask whether there are enough people in the system who want to have that kind of experience. There are, in fact, many others who quite legitimately want to be trained to do a different kind of job and to go to an institution which will provide that training in the shortest, most direct, way – to join an in-house programme with their company, for example. Interest and the demand are actually very important and the point Leslie Wagner has made in a different context – that the Government has created a demand situation – is important. We have to ask – and this is where standards come in – not whether people are qualified to come in, but whether they have the capacity to benefit from the course in question and, if not, whether there is another course that we could reasonably and efficiently devise that would give them the development and the kind of education they want. And there you move from academic judgements to resource questions, and the situation becomes more complex. I don't think there is a natural limit at 30%, because you can find plenty of cases of people who develop late and wish to take up the opportunity later.

Stephen Hope (Rector, Roehampton Institute): Do you think that there is a minimum period of time over which to acquire the knowledge and understanding required for a university degree and, if so, what is that period of time?

Professor Sutherland: If we are talking about producing graduates who, at the end of a given period of study, are genuinely educated in their subjects, we clearly look to find detailed knowledge of aspects of the subject, a grasp of the methods being used, an understanding of how far the subject has got and where, eventually, it might lead. In the case of many of our students, especially 18 year-olds, there is also a maturing process going on. I think that they will not reach the necessary degree of understanding in periods shorter than three years. That is already very short by international standards. But the controlling question is what counts as being educated. I have known many mature students, particularly in some of the humanities subjects, who have brought to their studies a wealth of experience and reading and understanding, that would make it quite conceivable that they could complete, in a shorter period, the kind of educational process that younger students take an extra year over. Practical questions come into this as well. Education is very expensive and we should be doing what we can to minimise the time, and therefore the expense, for those who do not qualify for a grant. The underlying question is whether the individual will be educated in the broader sense I have tried to outline.

2
One Industrialist's Views
Sir Graham Day, Chairman, Cadbury Schweppes plc

I welcome this opportunity to contribute to the discussion concerning universities in the twenty-first century. I do not say this as mere politeness. Rather, I say it very sincerely as one who, through some thirty-seven years of post-graduation employment has perceived, increasingly, an apparent lack of strategy and direction on the part of too many universities. For universities, and the public purse which provides much of their funding, the new century serves as a useful focal point in the establishing of longer term goals and the formulation of strategies to realise those goals. I have drawn the conclusion, hopefully a correct one, that this series of lectures may form some part of the strategy formulation process for British universities.

I have styled these remarks 'one industrialist's views'. Following my early years as a practising barrister, I have spent some twenty five years in industry, mainly in Britain, and, for over fifteen years of that twenty-five, have been at the apex of various industrial corporate pyramids. Thus, I am indeed an industrialist, in the managerial sense, and it is with that industrial background and perspective that I have been invited to speak to you this evening.

It would be reasonable for you to wonder whether, in addition to my industrial persona, there are any other elements in my life which may bear on the subject I will be discussing and which, perhaps, contribute to any biases I may reveal.

In the 1950s, I spent five years at Dalhousie University in Halifax, Nova Scotia, Canada, first studying history and political science and then going on to that university's law school. As you will know, in Canada, unlike the United Kingdom, Law Schools are post-graduate institutions, and the possession of an undergraduate qualification is a prerequisite for entry. In 1977 I returned to Dalhousie as a

21

professor in the post-graduate business school. I taught for four years and, concurrently, headed a policy research centre. In 1980, I entered a doctoral programme at the University of Wales, but was lured back into the industrial world without having completed.

You should know, also, that my elder daughter is an academic, teaching in a post-graduate educational psychology programme at a Canadian university. While she might take exception to some of the views which I will express, I must acknowledge that a number of my attitudes have been influenced by her experience and comment.

Finally, over the last decade I have spent much of my time and some of my money, and directed significant corporate funds, in support of various British universities. The personal motivation and the corporate commitment share an identical conviction: that the performance of our universities and their graduates significantly determine how British business and the British nation perform in economic terms, and have obvious social implications.

There are two, perhaps obvious, caveats I should register. The first is that while, over the last nine years or so, I have been involved with a number of British universities, including some recently granted that status, I am not a British university 'insider'. Neither can I claim to be a long-term, systematic observer of universities.

Strategy

I said that over time I perceived an apparent lack of strategy and direction on the part of too many universities. It is only fair I should say also that, in my view, successive governments and their appointed agencies have done little to remedy this shortcoming. Short-term tactics dressed up as strategies deceive few. Certainly some universities, within the limits of their respective operational realities, manifestly have strategic thrusts.

These would appear to be a minority. What I see is a pattern of year-on-year tactical activity which seems to address some real and some imagined imperatives other than the interests of universities' customers – the students, and their customers' customers – the employers of graduates.

As the strategic goal for the twenty-first century I would propose that universities should attract, educate, train and graduate increasing numbers of persons with qualifications required for post-graduation employment. In commenting on five elements which, I believe, touch upon this proposed goal, I admit selectivity and make no pretensions of comprehensiveness.

Post-Graduation Employment

While I respect, and sometimes envy, those who are able to combine a preferred course of study with subsequent directly related employment, my judgement is that for many this combination is not on offer. I say this with some personal insight. Had I been able to indulge my own under-graduate preferences, I would have continued either as a not very good musician or as a dilettante historian. Economics, the personal kind, fortunately denied me these indulgences.

In Britain, with the State as education's prime funder, it is reasonable, to my mind, that something should be expected in return. That return should be that graduates secure a qualification which is relevant to employment opportunities. Because I see British industrial and commercial competitiveness as the issue now and in the early years of the next century, university graduates with needed competences are critical to enhancing that competitiveness. In order to help secure those competences, I would seek to influence choice of programme as students seek university entrance.

This could be achieved primarily through support funding and tuition fee mechanisms. To take the extreme, I would graduate tuition costs downwards, including to zero, for well qualified students entering and successfully progressing to degrees which are considered to be in national demand. Similarly, I would vary central government funding so as to provide financial incentives for universities to focus more on degree programmes for which employment demand is considered to exist.

On the other hand, I would levy higher fees to be paid by students where such demand was not apparent. For some, perhaps many, sociology, for example, may be an appealing course of study. However with an employment demand for, say, mathematics and physics, some incentives to reconsider seem indicated. Exceptions could be made for exceptional students seeking to study for degrees where the demand was minimal. I acknowledge that it would be necessary to take into account the preservation and continuation of programmes which underpin university study generally and also areas of excellence where demand may be modest.

I do not pretend to be well informed on the subject of university fees and government support funding. Equally, I must acknowledge that it is not possible for me to assess the impact of any such policies on the costs to central government and the finances of universities. While net costs and financial benefits are central to the adoption and implementation of any policy, I seek here only to suggest structural finance possibilities which might help deliver a desired strategic objective.

In any discussion on education – primary, secondary, under-graduate or graduate – my overwhelming interest is in fitness for employment. The ability first to secure a job, then to hold or change it while continuing always to learn and to adapt constructively to change, is something we should encourage our graduates to develop and our educators to promote.

In the context of twenty-first century universities, the need for post-secondary education to produce employable graduates, and in greater numbers, can only grow. There is the related dimension that when a nation exhibits an education culture, and the results to prove it, inward investment follows with associated benefits.

My topic for this evening is not one which naturally gives rise to a discussion of British attitudes towards education in general. Nevertheless, let me briefly recount a personal anecdote which illustrates one attitude that, in my view, continues to colour how too many view a university education. The circumstances are not important, but in the mid nineteen eighties a rather senior estab-lishment figure enquired, quite politely, whether I had had one of those North American 'applied' university educations. I sensed his use of the word 'education' was a concession, but refraining from referring to my six years of compulsory Latin etc., I replied, equally politely, that he was quite correct as I had always known that I would have to work for a living. There continues to be a reluctance, on the part of some parents, students, universities and employers, to relate education to securing subsequent employment.

Easier Admission

Nothing which I have experienced or observed in the whole of my adult life has lessened my conviction that we require more of our young to complete school, to go on to university and in so doing to acquire those attributes which will enable individuals to serve themselves and society. In my suggested strategic goal for twenty-first century universities, I use the words 'increasing numbers'. I hope no-one will disagree with the premise that Britain requires a higher percentage of its population to be university graduates. Assuming this is so, the basic and, I believe, the continuing problem, is the failure to have enough of our youth complete school. This fact must be taken into account as plans are developed for twenty-first century British universities.

Understandably, and quite properly, universities are places of 'higher education' to which we progress having completed school, to a standard, and with courses which purport to qualify us for university admission. For the great majority of university applicants this route will probably continue to be proper and relevant. However, there are people – how large in number I cannot say – who for a variety of reasons do not fit this pattern easily, or at all. The social, and perhaps moral, question is: should they be denied university admission? I say no. The Open University and some conventional universities have gone quite a way toward facilitating university admission for what may be described as 'mature' students. We need, and will need, more of this. Making a university education possible for many more citizens is one of the major challenges for our universities in the twenty-first century.

Some possible mechanisms occur to me. Starting with entrance examinations, universities would determine the actual level of a would-be student's preparedness. Such entrance examination would be a substitute for recognised school completion documentation. To the extent – and this would be expected – that entrance examinations exposed deficiencies, the applicant could be referred to make-up courses, including non-credit university courses. If the differences were modest, conditional university entrance might be granted, dependent upon the successful completion of make-up courses and progress in university courses proper.

The good news, upon which we can build, is that some universities are facilitating the entry of mature students and have assisted them to remedy their deficient admission requirements. The not-so-good news is that the numbers involved are modest and that non-conventional university entrance remains difficult.

The objective for twenty-first century British universities would be to appeal to the widest possible cross-section of the population. The door to higher education, and thus one important route to improving the quality of life for individuals, with corresponding national benefit, should be not merely ajar, but wide open. In short, I advocate a considerable lessening of the rigidity, *de facto* and *de jure*, of university admission requirements.

On the other hand, I would move to tighten the graduation criteria. I would argue for 'easier in – harder out' university standards. In the real world, marginal graduates fail themselves, their unfortunate employers, and the institutions who graduate them.

Satisfying the Customer

Somewhat belatedly, but with acceleration, most of us in industry and commerce have recognised that satisfying customers is, ultimately, that characteristic which determines our successes. My perception is that the recognition by universities that students are customers is uneven. Some universities, of course, consider they 'know what is best': others appear to be student volume driven. Some universities, or more properly some faculties and departments, exhibit commendably high levels of commitment to their student customers. I am not suggesting by any means that universities should pander to their customers – by and large young – but that, overall, universities must become more interested in and dedicated to the academic and employment fortunes of the average student.

The human excellence which British universities have produced, and which they continue to graduate, reflects credit on prior schooling, the capability of the students themselves, their instructors and, of course, the universities. We should all be poorer if this excellence were not to continue. However, the pursuit of excellence for the very capable few, who are so satisfying to teach, is not an alternative to a better deal for the average. Surely, as we prepare for the next century, it should be possible to redirect more of the attention of university management, planners, funders and faculty toward the average, and not just the best. The excellent minority, no matter how meritorious, does not and will not address the national requirement for significantly greater numbers of adequately educated and trained university graduates. Let us, then, preserve the one and enhance the other.

There is a biased view, without much if any data, that there exists a clear universities' 'pecking order' from which conclusions can be drawn as to the quality of the degree awarded to graduates. It may be true that good schools produce good university candidates and that inadequate universities may not damage good students. Nevertheless, my experience is that in the graduate recruitment process, it is essential for employers to create and operate dispassionately, over time, a rankings list of universities based on employers' cumulative knowledge of the graduates hired. Imperfect though this may be, the evidence available to me over two decades in Britain is that the traditional demarcation of universities severally described as ancient, long-established, new and former polytechnics is a poor indication of likely graduate adequacy.

Teaching Versus Research

Research and teaching are equally important parts of a whole university. On a personal level, research enables some talented individuals to express themselves creatively and in so doing to advance our knowledge, save or enhance the expectation of life, ease our working tasks and generally contribute to our national well-being. Universities have long provided homes for research and researchers. In the twenty-first century it should be no different.

Research will continue to be funded by the State on behalf of us all, by altruistic benefactors and charitable institutions, and by properly self-seeking industrial concerns. I have a single caution. As government research funding may provide critical base finance, care must be taken to ensure that current perceptions of research capability do not operate so as to shut out future potential through funding criteria which are too narrow.

As with graduate excellence, some British university research is world class and absolutely must be preserved. I have no problem whatsoever with research in its various guises in the university world.

My problem – and both personally and corporately I have one – is that too often teaching is subordinated to research – research which, variously, may be excellent, good or indifferent.

I consider it axiomatic that a number of researchers are competent teachers, especially at the post-graduate level. Indeed, it would be surprising if this were not true. However, I fear that too many university teachers whose vocation and skills are primarily pedagogic are forced into pseudo-research in order to secure employment, promotion and, ultimately, university tenure. I distinguish, of course, those teachers who work to keep up to date, and write to report their studies or create teaching texts, from those who are driven into research by the system. There are many motivations for university faculty to 'research' – I place the word in quotation marks deliberately. Raising money for the institution and, of course, the individual, features prominently. And, for the institution, there is the apparent need to be seen as a successful place of research in order to enhance wider funding potential.

Those who view themselves primarily as researchers should not be compelled to teach. In such instances, let the appropriateness of the research and its quality be judged by the usual criteria and funded accordingly by state or private sponsor. Equally, let those who would be teachers teach and free them from the research and publish-or-perish necessity. In return, such study and reporting as may be necessary, at a minimum, to remain abreast of developments in their respective fields should be demonstrated regularly. Student customers deserve skilled and committed teachers. University teaching should be, and be seen to be, a valued career in itself.

Who Manages?

A virtue ascribed to universities is that they are radical in thought, but not in deed. I would subscribe to radicalism in thought being a university virtue and one which, in our society, is made possible by the traditional freedom enjoyed by universities and their faculties. However, that valued individual independence in thought and expression operates to clog the veins of universities as institutions.

I do not see that management of the university as an institution should be a reciprocal of the individualism implicit in university academic life. In other words, I see no conflict between a university management which manages because it must – certainly not by committee – and the proper continuation of freedom of academic expression. Obviously, effective university leadership requires, as elsewhere, efforts toward securing 'hearts and minds'. But there is no escaping the necessity for management to manage. Universities are not different in this regard. University managers can expect that virtually any initiative may be countered by an academic claiming trespass on his or her rights and freedoms. It is the academic rights and freedoms themselves which must be preserved, however, not a preference for a particular course of managerial action or inaction.

As we in industry and commerce know, change is a constant. Above all, we seek to manage change positively and effectively: with the grain if we can, against it if we must. I do not consider universities to be exempt from this reality. Thus, universities in their governance must be freed from internal committee-led, consensus-driven constraints, and encouraged, indeed required, to be less evolutionary and more radical.

Moreover, not only does delay frustrate the attainment of strategic goals, delay is invariably expensive. Therefore, I would add alacrity to radicalism in university management. Simply do what must be done, and do it faster!

While I am critical of the apparent lack of strategy within and for many universities, I must acknowledge the structural constraints which inhibit the process. Perhaps if universities' managements were freer to manage, they would be better able to contend with the possibilities of the next century and thereby serve their customers, broaden their appeal and play the critical role in society and the economy which I believe is their responsibility.

A final word. In organisational terms, most universities are mature and, as such, have well developed structures and processes, as do the Government agencies which relate to universities. Structures and processes are not unimportant. Provided they are intended to function as part of the strategy delivery system, organisation, structure and process can assist the solution instead of contributing to the problem.

However, for the twenty-first century, the agenda must not be about structures and processes as ends in themselves. The future agenda must be about people: the student customers, their needs and what, as graduates, they can contribute, including to their employers.

Discussion

Baroness Perry of Southwark: You have spoken of a need for all higher education to be related to employment and the needs of employers. You then seemed to rule various courses in or out of that category. The Rector of the University of Vilnius in Lithuania recently spoke, brilliantly and most movingly, about the relationship between universities and employment. He pointed out that there was no market in a country, like his, emerging from chaos following the break up of the former Soviet Union. There was an economy which was entirely centrally managed, where nobody knew how to be entrepreneurial and many lacked basic skills. There had been no modernisation. In countries like his there had been politicians whose prime, necessary qualification was that they were uneducated. There had been a civil service which was entirely politicised, with a very low level of education and which was wholly corrupt. He went on to say that his job at the university was not only to create highly qualified engineers, technologists, people who know about management, commerce and enterprise, but also to create people who are humanists. In his view, we, in the West, take for granted our PPE degrees and degrees in philosophy and ancient history and so on. He sees courses such as these providing the background for the incorruptible, thoughtful, highly intelligent and intellectual politicians, civil servants and local government people whom we have, but which the countries of Eastern Europe have to create from nothing.

What the Vilnius Rector gave was a picture of the total job of the higher education system. It is more than simply the production of people who are hotel managers, engineers and lawyers – the obvious raft of people who have done vocational courses. It is also the purpose of universities to provide a cadre of people who are needed in employment to create a civilised society and who have studied 'useless' subjects – and I speak as a philosopher – like philosophy and sociology. Do you think you are in danger of defining employment too narrowly?

Sir Graham: No. I think you have attempted to define employment. I would accept totally for example that civil servants are employed. What I said was that it seemed that more people were studying sociology than there were positions for sociologists, or than there were for those who used sociology as a springboard for social work.

I am not attempting in any way to shut out vocations, including intellectual vocations. But there remains a gulf to be bridged where what is perceived as education is totally unlinked to subsequent employment. I am looking for a better mix. It is very disquieting to see not inconsiderable numbers of graduates – last year's crop, some from the year before – who do not have the skills necessary to secure the employment which they would prefer. The problem is that there is a mismatch between the graduate ability recognised by the degree and the employment market. If graduates wish to be philosophers, civil servants, whatever the mix may be, that is fine. If graduates with a philosophy degree then come to me and say: 'Please, we would like to be in the power generation business or marketing', then I want to know how many statistical courses they have had. It is the mismatch that bothers me.

Professor Gareth Williams (Institute of Education, University of London): I would like to press you on the question of the relationship between higher education and employment and to see how far you would be willing to go in linking the two. The economy fluctuates and tends to want different kinds of graduates at different times, and it takes a long time to produce a graduate. How far would you be prepared to go down the road of manpower planning in order to secure the kind of higher education system that you want.

Sir Graham: I wonder whether the fluctuations are as real as is sometimes alleged. For example, I believe there has been a fairly consistent demand for people coming out of universities with a fairly wide range of quantitative skills. Physics and maths are useful examples because they are not specifically employment-related; they do, however, provide a significant base of quantitative skills which enable the first degree graduate then to accept a high level of subsequent job-related preparation. Within fairly broad areas there is constancy in demand. In the Chartered Accountancy profession in Scotland, for example, admission to the qualifying programme requires the possession of a relevant degree. The word 'relevant" is interesting. Relevant degrees include economics, business studies and, again, quantitative degrees like maths. In England and Wales, however, the requirement is simply for a degree. There is no suggestion that those who have studied religion or history, for example, make poor accountants. They do not. But there is a much greater river for them to bridge.

I am not saying that we should estimate the number of sociologists which we require. That is much too narrow. The mesh is too fine. But I would argue that, if the debate were joined, it would be part of self-planning, including at school level, to say to people: 'You are actually going to have to work for a living, so please, as you think ahead, prepare accordingly.'

Susan Gey (City Technology Colleges Trust): You seem to be painting a picture of universities as rather reactive in terms of their responsibility to provide people fit for employment. I would be interested in knowing how you view the universities' role in encouraging creative, innovative, entrepreneurial people who can then go out, start new businesses and, therefore, create new employment for others.

Sir Graham: I can cite, as an example of an entrepreneur, a young man whom I first met when he was at Cambridge. He had formed an organisation there directed towards entrepreneurism. He graduated, went to work, did his MBA at Harvard and is now back. He is absolutely fixed on being in some kind of entrepreneurial activity, either by himself or with a small organisation. That fits my view of the world. Universities provide an enabling function. They can suggest or tailor certain courses in order to enhance the skills in question. At least the student, or prospective student, is being urged to think about what he or she wants to do with their lives. Do not wait until someone presses the diploma into your hand and then say: 'Here I am. Employ me.' Whatever the focus may be, most of us have to work. Please think about work and then do something which as near as possible will fit you for something you think you would like to do, or at least are prepared to do.

Professor John Davidson (Vice-Master, Trinity College, Cambridge) I support the idea of long-term planning but this is needed by industry as well as universities. There is a cyclical phenomenon in the graduate employment market. In times of boom, when investment is high and plant is being built, industrial recruiters visit my department and want as many chemical engineers as they can get. Then the industrial cycle turns down about three or four years later and, if the recruiters come at all, they want someone with a first class degree and managing director potential. This switches the students off. The result is that there is a reduced intake of students. Then, three or four years later the boom comes back again. Certainly we ought to have long term planning in the universities but it requires equally long term recruiting policies by industry so that supply and demand are matched.

Sir Graham: I absolutely agree.

David Thorpe (English Speaking Union): You implied that, in some ways, graduation should be more difficult. Perhaps you could comment on that in the international context, because I understand that drop-out rates overseas are higher. Could you also comment on your view that preparedness for entering university should be looked at.

Sir Graham: What I want is 'easier in and harder out'. It is difficult to look at courses in isolation. I would advocate, for example, adding an extra year to some programmes where three years is inadequate. I would actually like university graduates – with no exceptions – to be able to write and to read so that they actually comprehend. I have run across more than the occasional university graduate who lacks the basic reading, writing and adding up skills.

I also want to open the doors. There was a young man who worked as a semi-skilled assembler for the car line at Cowley when I was at Rover. We decided to inventory the totality of our human resources and, with the employees' permission we, among other things, ran IQ tests. This young man's test was virtually off the scale. When you looked at him he was about 20, rising 21, had been married, divorced and had spent some time at Her Majesty's pleasure. He was not a particularly committed employee. However, if I were as bright as he was, I would not find car line work the most stimulating vocation either. But, that young man now has a master's degree. He is a very good employee and is making a very significant personal and national contribution.

The point is that, as a willing, adaptable organisation, we were able to provide a way forward for this young man and I am arguing for a broadening of the 'capture' area. Statistically it may increase the fall-out percentages but that does not worry me a great deal. I think it would lift the output at the other end. But equally I am keen that exit standards should, at worst, not be lessened and, at best, be progressively hardened and tightened.

Robert Hinds (Institute of Mathematics and its Applications): My institute is dedicated to the applied aspects of mathematics rather than to the pure. Schools are now taking a broader approach to the teaching of maths, and so it is harder to get people through a maths degree in the short time of three years. There is a need for four-year courses. But there is a funding problem, and a danger, at a time when we need twice as many maths graduates, that the Government will say we can only produce three quarters as many students if we have four year courses.

A few years ago there were serious problems in recruiting mathematics graduates into teacher training. Now it is overflowing, and the reason is that the jobs in industry are not there, and young people are turning to teaching for security. This is good news for the schools if the situation is managed properly. But there is a mismatch in the forward planning in the employment and education sectors. What can be done about this?

Sir Graham: Having signed off the Schoolteachers' Review Body report recently I am currently very aware of the mismatch and also of the influx of people into the teaching profession who perhaps at a different time and in a different economic environment might not have elected that as a vocation. The forecasting sins are not only those of universities and business. They also include the Department for Education. Its forecast of places in teaching preparation was wildly out, and a lot of the financing for education is, in my view, very short-term.

Taking maths and physics as an example, because they are so fundamental to a wide range of employment potential, it seems to me that whether the graduate elects to go into Teachers' College or, at another time, to work in manufacturing industry or some other kind of employment, the significant thing is that a person with those degrees has options. School teaching may not be their first choice but they are employable. It really underlines the point: there are alternatives because the subject of the degree opens up a range of employment possibilities. There are those with other degrees in other subjects who do not enjoy that range of options.

I share your concern with the broader question of how to attract and find the funding for more people in these particular subjects. In most sophisticated manufacturing today, if the operators do not have a basic ability in differential and integral calculus – not necessarily sitting down and working out equations, but understanding them – then they cannot comprehend the machines and the operations of the machines which confront them. Even at a pretty basic manufacturing level, maths up to that level is now essential for day to day operations on the shop floor.

Martin Tims (Manager, Education Programmes, Esso UK): Some of the studies that I have been looking at recently show that school children, in particular, and even university students have an antipathy towards a management career. They say they are chemical engineers or physicists and the last thing they want to do is to become a manager. How can we encourage them to recognise the skills you need for management and then to go on and study them?

Sir Graham: It says so much about attitudes. A number of those attitudes get transmitted, in the home, through the schools, perhaps the universities – variations of 'don't put your daughter on the stage, Mrs Worthington.' It takes time to change attitudes towards industry. I hope you might agree that attitudes towards industry, business and management are more positive today than twenty years ago. I certainly perceive them to be more positive. At my last count there were at least 92 MBA granting institutions in the UK. They are a pretty mixed lot. But the very fact that they exist and students apply, are admitted and ultimately graduate, indicates that there is a demand for business and industry-related management skills which did not exist twenty years ago, when the first two major business schools in the country started.

I think that precept and example are very important, and some careers – or callings – are in favour and others are not. When people in business find themselves in the High Court then we are all diminished thereby. The same applies to other professions, but business frauds are fairly major ones – businesses collapse – and that is factored into judgement. But I think the whole question of management is now accepted. I would say that I am a professional manager. That is probably accepted as a vocation today. I don't think it would have been twenty years ago.

Professor Marion Hicks (Director, United Biscuits (UK)): I have been in industry for six years after thirty years as a teacher and researcher in the University of London. I also chair the South West Thames Regional Health Authority. I have progressed from a career where I have been producing and educating graduates to one where I am very much concerned with employing them. The dichotomy between industry and higher education is still there and it is due not only to the attitude of the academics to the industrial world. It is also the other way. The thing that struck me very forcibly six years ago was that I had moved from an environment where they used my title of professor with respect, to one where they only call me professor when they are trying to be unpleasant. Industry has an attitude to academics which is just as firm as academics to industry.

You talked of a mismatch between university education and the requirements of industry. Interestingly you didn't touch on what I find to be the biggest mismatch. I am less worried about an individual's knowledge and skills base than you are because I believe those can be acquired. I am much more worried about personal attitudes and ability to work with other people. At the moment the traditional education system in this country is not serving the country's industry to best advantage because it is entirely built round development of the individual and the development of excellence. I am torn here because, as an academic, I like to think of universities as the repositories of excellence and the places where you really must develop excellence in individuals and push back the frontiers of knowledge. But the minute you go into industry the one thing you know is that you do not want an individual. What you want is a team worker. And the one thing our traditional education system has entirely failed to develop is any ability to work in teams.

In my Health Service job, I now realise it is not just a malaise of industry. It is very much a malaise of government as well. Government is built on individuals and I really honestly believe that where you have departments, where there happen to be six ministers or junior ministers, you have six individuals and six individual agendas, and not a team. This is the result of our education. Education develops individuals who rise to the top by their ability to derive from other people, to take other people's results and apply them and use them. But one thing they come out of our education system entirely lacking is the ability to integrate, work as a team and realise that five people working together equals seven, whereas five people working as individuals equals three in terms of effectiveness. This, to me, is the biggest mismatch in our higher education system and university requirements.

Sir Graham: I agree, but the situation is not unique to the United Kingdom. I suspect that it is common, at least to the English speaking world. I find myself envying the Japanese because, education aside, they have virtually a team culture. Historically, I am told it is known as the rice-growing culture because you cannot grow rice by yourself. You have to have your neighbours muck in to help you.

It is very difficult to take individuals out of the system and determine whether they can or will function as a team. I am always interested in asking graduates whether they have played team sports, for example. One looks for evidence of an ability to interact, some evidence of latent interpersonal skills. But it is a problem.

Not the least of the things business schools can do is to thrust groups of people together and force them willy-nilly to perform as a unit. Even if that unit performs badly it is a learning experience for those who are thrust together. And I strive for situations, albeit artificial, where you are forcing interaction before there is something really valuable at issue, to try to develop it. But, in due course, the organisation sloughs off people who cannot bring themselves within the larger net.

Professor Peter Mortimore (Institute of Education, University of London): Perhaps you could draw on your own experience and speculate a little about the future. What is the likely impact on the university of the future of information technology and the opportunities for groups, networks and individuals to link up and to get access to information, to expert systems, and to virtual reality?

Sir Graham: Everything which impacts on society at large will affect universities. They are not islands. And of course it will change the culture. Not the least of things which may be negative is that the individualism referred to earlier can actually be enhanced by working in some of these areas because you don't require human interaction in order to progress your particular bit of work. Of course, there are many positive benefits and they are already happening, but we have to be concerned about anything which dehumanises our activities.

John Guy (Principal, The Sixth Form College, Farnborough): We have the task in my college both of sending people on to higher education and of employing them once they have been there. I suppose, therefore, I have many sympathies with your view of 'easier in and harder out'. As an employer, I see youngsters coming from higher education with something called an upper second class degree and I don't really understand what that is. Could you comment on criteria for first degree level, and on quality assurance in the HE sector.

Sir Graham:I have referred to employers running, over time, an informal, private ranking of degrees by subject. It is very hard to do that from the outset. Over a period it is very helpful, if not precise. I will give a positive example. In a particular situation there are two candidates. Candidate One, from a university has an upper second class degree. Candidate Two is from a former polytechnic. The job requires fairly good quantitative skills. According to the ready reckoner of this particular employer, the poly degree is a factor of 2.7 better than the same classification of degree from the university.

I don't know any other way around it, because while a number of universities, officially or unofficially, have been running quality control/quality assurance programmes – and we are now, I understand, moving into a mandatory or quasi-mandatory regime for this purpose – all graduates, all degrees, although apparently the same, are not equal. I have told you how I operate and I find other people operating the same way. Now, there is bias in that and also, over time, you fail to adjust, except in the light of *ex post facto* experience. Universities change. They get better or worse. Comparatives change, so your system is imperfect. However, if you do not have a system, you have nothing.

Brian Gomes da Costa (Bath College of Higher Education): I want to ask a historical question. In 1966/67 the Colleges of Advanced Technology – an interesting piece of British social engineering – were transmogrified into something else. In 1992/93 the binary line was abolished. Does that contribute to the solution of the ranking problem or has it exacerbated it?

Sir Graham: In terms of immediate perception, from the point of view of the recruiter, I do not think there has been a change. But inclusion of other organisations in the university net has actually helped, because many former polytechnics have cultures which are more in line with my needs as an employer. They also have a flexibility in dealing with part-time and mature students, who can make very desirable employees. As a hiring employer I have always found myself very much in tune with what a lot of the former polytechnics were and are doing. I don't think the change of name has done anything except, over time, maybe make them feel better about themselves and eliminated a perceptual difference – which is not unimportant for the graduates. On balance I think it is a good thing.

3

The Research Mission and Research Manpower

Sir David Phillips, KBE, FRS, Chairman of the Advisory Board for the Research Councils

I take some pleasure in coming to speak to you on the subject of the research mission in universities when it is only recently that the Advisory Board for the Research Councils (ABRC) published its Advice to the Chancellor of the Duchy of Lancaster on the White Paper on Science and Technology. Not only does our document give me fuel for this speech, but it also takes me back to a previous strategy document from the Board, our *Strategy for the Science Base*, which was published in 1987 – to some consternation I seem to remember. I hope I can be as provocative today.

The task you have set me is to make some predictions about the future of universities in the twenty-first century. That is clearly very difficult, particularly if I were so rash as to attempt a long-range prediction. Instead I shall follow Newman in attempting only one step – or perhaps two – and, despite Burke's warning that 'you can never plan the future by the past', I shall adopt the sentiment of T S Eliot that:

Time present and time past
Are both perhaps present in time future,
And time future contained in time past.

In looking at times past, present and future, I shall reflect on the emergence of the research mission in universities, and attempt to characterise the diverse sources of funding for universities, concentrating on that for research. I shall describe the developing relationship between universities and their funders in terms of purchasers and providers of goods and services. Turning to the

39

internal management of resources in universities, I shall try to characterise the challenges facing senior university management. In
particular, I shall dwell upon the need to provide structures to
produce the necessary critical mass of research activity to support
high quality investigation, and to facilitate interdisciplinary research,
whilst meeting the country's need for greater output of highly-
trained manpower. Finally, I shall draw attention to the personnel
challenge in universities; in particular, the need for longer-term
planning in the creation and development of the research workforce.

Time Past

Let us begin by reflecting a little on times past. We sometimes forget
that the very first universities, in twelfth-century Italy, were very
much market-led teaching institutions. The modern research-focused
university emerged in the nineteenth century in Germany. Its key
strengths were the establishment of the research laboratory which
concentrated the critical resources necessary for forefront research;
the organisation of research around a powerful professor with his
team; and the strong attention given to the rigorous training of
new researchers. Some argue that it had its weaknesses too, in its
arrangement along single discipline lines but, by way of contrast,
it is interesting to note that the Professor of Physics in Oxford in
1914 remarked: '… the wish to do research betrays a certain rest-
lessness of mind'.

Although there had been much debate on the subject from the
middle of the nineteenth century, and a modest beginning in the
National Physical Laboratory for example, it was war – the first and
second World Wars – which brought home the need for public
investment in research in the UK. And such public investment was
always linked to the need to underpin industry and the economy.
Consider, for example, the following statement:

> There is a strong consensus of opinion among persons engaged both
> in science and in industry that a special need exists at the present
> time for new machinery and for additional State assistance in order
> to promote and organise scientific research with a view especially to
> its application to trade and industry.

You may be surprised to learn that it comes from a statement by the Board of Education to the Houses of Parliament on the establishment of the Department for Scientific and Industrial Research in 1916 and not from the White Paper on Science and Technology in 1993.

Public investment in science went hand in hand with the need to increase the stock of highly-qualified manpower in the economy. Figure 1 shows the growth in the numbers of students in universities since before the second World War: it shows quite clearly the rapid growth rates in the late sixties and early seventies following the foundation of the new universities and the substantial increases over the last years.

Figure 1 University Student Numbers, 1939–1991, UK

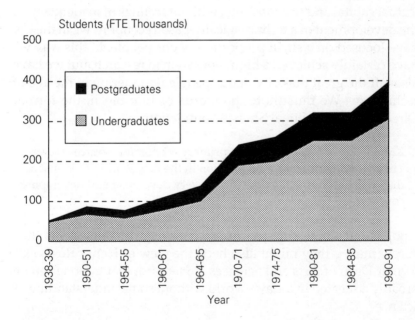

Furthermore, it is most important to recognise that this covers only the old university sector and that, by 1990-91, there were also more than 350,000 full-time equivalent (FTE) students in the former Polytechnics and Colleges Funding Council (PCFC) sector, which was, by then, producing more graduates than the old universities.

Clearly we must pay tribute to the role of polytechnics in rejuvenating the skills base of the country. They provide somewhat more than fifty per cent of further and higher education, and have excelled in the highly efficient provision of a diversity of training opportunities for a multitude of people. Technological universities, of course, have an honourable tradition – beginning in 1794 with the Ecole Polytechnique in France. In this country, that mantle has fallen largely on the polytechnics. It is much to be hoped that, with their new status, they remain true to that tradition.

While my main concern is the research mission, I cannot emphasise too strongly the complementary importance of the teaching mission conducted in the university and polytechnic systems. Whereas the US and German systems of higher education have been successful, in the past, in providing high-level education and training to enable a large proportion of their people to make the most of their intellectual capital and to contribute, without feelings of inadequacy, to the development of a technologically-based economy, we in the UK have focused on a small proportion of our people. In this way we have certainly achieved a high reputation in research, but we have also left the great majority of our people floundering in the age of technology. We must note the words of Eric Bloch, the former Director of the National Science Foundation:

> Knowledge and people are the primary economic resources today. They will determine the US position in the new world order, just as they will determine the position of every developed and developing country.

And, as our universities re-design their degree courses – as they surely must – they might also heed the view of Henry Rosovsky, former Dean of Arts and Sciences at Harvard, that 'no-one can be broadly educated in today's world without some understanding of science.'

Some fear for the effects of mass higher education on the research mission. I can only repeat that it is not a matter of either/or for the country, but rather two essential strands for a successful modern society.

Time Present

Let us now turn to times present, and the current funding of universities. Figure 2 illustrates the various funding streams in the old university sector, and the change which occurred in the mix between 1980 and 1990. The block grant fell from 59% in 1980, to 44% in 1990, while research grants and research contract income expanded from 15% to 23% in the same period.

Figure 2 Sources of University Income

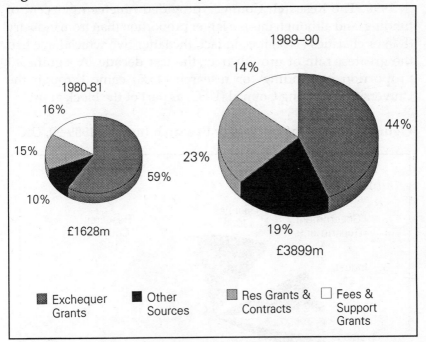

In very recent times, not reflected in this diagram, there has also been a shift in the balance of provision of funds for teaching from the unhypothecated grant towards student fees. So the overall picture is one of a shift from block grants toward specific recurrent funding of university activity; or, to put it in other words, toward universities earning their income through the provision of intellectual goods and services. This transition – toward the university gaining its income from its 'customers' – is an important one for university management, and one that is important for the future.

A similar picture can be painted of the former polytechnic sector. From a low base of £6m at the start of the 1980s, research income grew to £33m by the end of the decade: and receipts from the provision of other services doubled from £9m to £18m. At the same time, public funding – through the LEAs, the National Advisory Board, and then the PCFC – has grown, but with substantially greater productivity in the provision of higher and further education than that achieved by the old university sector.

Figure 3 looks at the specific funding of research in the old universities, and sets out the proportion of income from various sources in 1990. The Research Councils provided nineteen per cent of funding, and although this is a larger proportion than from industry (8%) or charities (11%) it is, in fact, the latter two which have had the greatest rate of growth over the last decade. A significant proportion of funding for research (45%) came through the Universities Funding Council (UFC) as part of the block grant.

Figure 3 Sources of University Research Income, 1989-90, UK

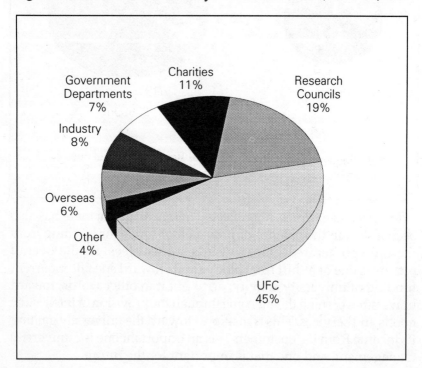

Recently I came across the announcement in *The Times* of 1953 of the Treasury grant to universities in that year. This was an interesting year because it saw the disappearance of earmarked grants in favour of general grants to institutions. The move was much approved by universities, who perceived it as important for the protection of their academic freedom. I am not so convinced. A problem of the unhypothecated block grant system was that it did not prompt universities to make calculations of how exactly resource was being deployed: broadly, between activity areas – teaching and research; but also narrowly, in terms of the costing of individual projects.

Following a recommendation in the ABRC 1987 strategy document, there has recently been a shift resources from the UFC to the Research Councils – the dual support transfer – so that the Research Councils now meet the full cost of the research they support (except for the salaries of permanent academic staff involved in the project, and the provision of the premises in which the research is conducted). This transfer has been important for two reasons. First, it is encouraging universities to cost more precisely the exact resource being deployed on a project or grant. Given the new mechanisms of funding for universities which I have elaborated, through the provision of educational and research goods and services, such accurate costing is vital to inform the appropriate pricing of contracts or consultancies. Second, the dual support transfer will allow clearer identification of where responsibilities lie in relation to the support of projects. While universities think, I am sure, that they are getting a hard deal from exercises which require that resource is more firmly defined in relation to activity, in the long run it should also help them to claim the appropriate resources for the services which they provide.

Those who have read the ABRC White Paper document will know that we drew back from recommending that the responsibility for staff salaries and premises should also be transferred to the Research Councils – though, even under such a regime, the Funding Councils would retain sums to support seed-corn research and to underpin work commissioned by other funders. We appreciated the difficulties for institutions in adjusting to new climates of funding. Nevertheless, I think we must accept that the present position is still less than satisfactory and leads to accounting difficulties.

First, there is the requirement – increasingly emphasised – that resources must be accounted for so that the taxpayer and the nation can have more assurance of where their money is being spent. The Higher Education Funding Councils (HEFCs) now indicate to universities how the grant to them is made up – including the split between research and teaching – and has indicated that dipstick tests may be used to explore how these resources are being deployed within universities. I recognise that we need to get a good balance between institutional autonomy – giving university managements the freedom to develop their own particular corporate strategies – and accountability; but I do think that, at the national level, we have a much weaker story to tell when we cannot say with confidence what is being purchased from the public purse. For this reason, the new Funding Councils, who are at present discussing the issue, are likely to take further steps in improving accountability for the funds which they disburse.

Second, there is much discussion nowadays about the so-called level-playing field. Government departments, which draw on public funds when they seek research services to support their own particular missions, or as investment – through the Office of Science and Technology (OST) – in basic research, have a range of different places where they can get their goods. Universities are key providers, but there are also the Government research establishments, the Institutes of the Research Councils and a large number of contract research organisations. Customers need to know the full cost of research in universities if they are to make fair choices between rival contractors; or at the very least, the effect of the HEFC block grant on university tenders must be fully understood. And, universities must be concerned to recover the full costs of any contract research they undertake – unless there is a good reason for subsidising it from university resources. Even then, a prudent university would wish to know the full costs and the extent of the subsidy.

Alongside the changes in funding which I have just explored, there has been a revolution in the human resources of universities. Figure 4 focuses on the changes in the academic teaching and research staffs in the old university sector over the last decade. In 1980-81 the majority of academic staff were engaged in research and teaching, supported out of the universities' general funds. However, by 1990-91, we see a rather different picture. The numbers supported by universities to undertake both teaching and research have fallen noticeably and there have been increases in the numbers supported on contracts, particularly of those employed specifically as researchers. The number of contract researchers has more than doubled, from around 6,500 people at the beginning of the period, to some 14,000 people by the end. And the growth continues.

Figure 4 University Academic Staff, 1980-1991, UK

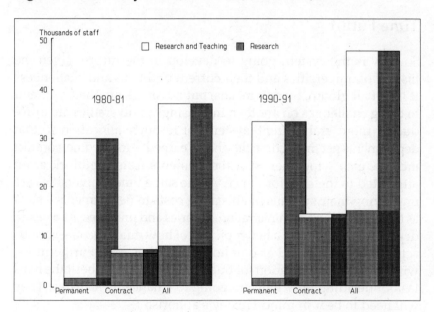

Much of the explanation for this phenomenon lies in the changing sources and mechanisms of funding in universities: particularly the transition from the unhypothecated block grant, to funding streams coming in piecemeal, and with less certainty, as the university supplies its various customers. A natural early reaction to this was to employ staff on short-term contracts to meet the specific terms of a particular grant or piece of commissioned work. Although it may be attractive to employ researchers for limited periods so as to ensure the appropriateness and vitality of those involved in a project, we also have to admit that fixed-term contracts are very useful for managers. They do not need to think far ahead about the portfolio of work that might be required; and they can vary their staffing – and in some departments staff costs may be as much as ninety per cent of the total cost of activities – at very short notice, according to their success, prevailing economic circumstances, or broader strategic considerations. Some such flexibility is essential for management, but perhaps too heavy a reliance on such measures smacks of inadequate planning.

Time Future

So how is the system going to develop in the future, given the history of universities and their current problems and challenges? It is not all gloom, by any means, but advances on one front tend to bring challenges on another. Increasingly, universities are intro- ducing more 'transparent' systems of resource allocation so that departments get the income they have 'earned' – fee income, contract income, etc., – together with the elements from the block grant attributed to their performance. At the same time, universities are improving their systems of allocating costs to departments – such as those for central administration, libraries and premises. As a result, departments will have a better picture of how much income various activities bring in, and also of how much they cost. Furthermore, with increasing delegation for budgeting, they will inherit the hard task of deciding how they are going to balance their books. They will need to bear in mind Huxley's aphorism:

> We all know how the size of sums of money appears to vary in a remarkable way according as they are being paid in or paid out.

On the whole, I welcome such movement toward local management which will, I believe, help in liberating the talented individual, though I have no doubt that the immediate reaction of departmen- tal heads is that they are overloaded with paper.

This brings us to the nature of the university itself, to the role of the institution as a whole and that of its senior management. Defining the particular mission or niche that the individual university is to fill in the highly diversified world of higher education; providing sufficient delegation to allow faculties, departments and centres to pursue their own creativity; ensuring that resources are properly accounted for, that departments are fully aware of the full costs of their activities, and that individual projects are fully costed and funded: all these will be very important. The key role, however, will be to ensure the quality of the institution's activities.

I want to emphasise, in particular, the importance of ensuring the high quality of the research mission, and the lessons we learned from the first – German – research universities:

- the need for concentration of research resources to maintain the high quality environment necessary for forefront investigation – the leading research laboratory;

- the need for a focus for individual research effort – so that research can gain a critical mass of people; and

- the need to maintain the connection with the training of the next generation of investigators.

Since I have been critical of the exercise in the past – and still have hopes for improvement – it is a pleasure here to pay tribute to the Research Assessment Exercise, initiated by the University Grants Committee (UGC) in 1986, and now completed for the third time by the UFC. There can be no doubt that this exercise has helped to sharpen university thinking about the research mission. Only today I noticed the following passage in the University of East Anglia News:

> There is widespread determination to move up a grade, and there is a wealth of ideas for consideration, ranging from early retirements and new blood, to the organisation of the undergraduate teaching timetable.

The news item goes on to mention a variety of measures that might be taken to improve the University's research ratings – including the sensible proposal that 'in some schools greater concentration on particular areas may be a way ahead'.

Such radical thinking must be good, but its value does rather depend upon whether the research ratings are measuring the attributes of research that we need to foster. The concerns here have centred on the temptation for people to work on short-term problems of little fundamental importance, the difficulty of giving proper credit to work at the applied end of the spectrum, and the problems of recognising and promoting inter-disciplinary work. All these are important concerns and I am sure that the Funding Councils will have them much in mind as they seek to improve the assessment process.

On the first, it is salutary to note the comment of Donald Kennedy, former President of Stanford University:

> The over-production of routine scholarship is one of the most egregious aspects of contemporary life. It tends to conceal really important work by its sheer volume, it wastes time and valuable resources.

On the second, I will note only that the false identification of applied research with near-market research – and hence its exclusion from public funding – has served to weaken further contacts between industry and the universities which badly need to be strengthened.

As for inter-disciplinary research, there can be no doubt of its importance. But, how best can it be managed in the context of discipline-based departments, concerned chiefly with undergraduate teaching? In 1938, Bernal commented on this increasing interdisciplinarity in *The Social Function of Science*, but added that:

> in practice inter-departmental jealousies are often stronger than common interests, and ... the result of this is an enormous lag in the appreciation of the relevance of one field of science to another.

I know well that the funding and organisation of inter-disciplinary research has always been difficult in universities, and I do fear that new methods of delegating budgets and identifying cost centres may make it even more difficult in the future to support such developments. How are such interstitial structures to be resourced under the new systems of transparent resource allocation?

Much has been talked recently about Graduate Schools. On the Continent, both the French and German governments have been investing in such structures in order to provide a lively and inter-disciplinary environment for research training. Universities in this country are also experimenting along these lines to provide an institutional focus for postgraduate education, to ease social isolation, promote structured training, and organise the particular administration of advanced education and training. These are tentative starts, but I think we will need to look more in the future to the American model of Graduate Schools. Here the Graduate School provides the focus not only for the organisation of postgraduate education, but also for research effort. It creates the critical mass for research, provides a calling point for users of research, and structures the use of human and financial resources toward the promotion of inter-disciplinary and path-breaking investigation. It is a remarkable fact that the great American research universities tend to have more graduate students than undergraduates. In Harvard, for example, there are some 6,500 graduates out of a total student population of 17,000, and there is at least one American University, the Rockefeller University, that has no undergraduates at all. I know that this arises from the nature of US degree courses but, as we move towards a similar system of mass higher education and increasing research concentration in major 'research universities', should we continue to ignore this model?

I do not want to be too prescriptive about how the research focus in universities should be maintained, but I do think that universities and Research Councils need to be partners in the development of research capacity, whatever form it takes. In our White Paper Advice we flagged some common objectives for higher education institutions (HEIs) and Councils:

- to foster mechanisms to support the most talented individuals wherever they work;

- to protect excellent work in small or isolated departments; and

- to identify and foster new and promising areas of science wherever they appear.

Furthermore, we recommended that the strategic partnerships between universities and Councils should involve longer-term support, and the creation of a 'recognised progression of support from grants to rolling programmes and thence to units and other selective, longer-term modes focused on the best scientists and clear scientific strengths'.

The last of these recommendations – on providing support to talented individuals through increasingly longer periods of support, culminating perhaps in a unit within an institution – seems particularly promising as a model for the future, and one that can provide the mechanism for the support of inter-disciplinary and dedicated research within systems of delegated budgeting and income generation. Perhaps such units can become the core of inter-disciplinary graduate schools, as these evolve over time.

Graduate schools could also play an important part in the development of a research personnel policy for universities in the future. A fairly fundamental re-think of how the human resources in the university are to be used and developed in the future is now required.

- *We need to look carefully at how many people we bring into higher training.* For example, how many should embark on a structured masters course to equip them for a wide range of destinations, or test their abilities in research; and how many should embark on higher research training – through the PhD and post-doctoral fellowships?

- *We need to look at the qualifications and training provided.* For instance, does the traditional PhD meet the needs of the various labour markets which will be the destinies of those qualifying in universities? In the halcyon days of the 1960s universities could consume virtually all their own products; but our new researchers go farther afield today. Are they best equipped for their multifarious tasks? A particular feature I would flag for the future will be much greater diversity in the siting of postgraduate education – with universities working with Science Base Institutes, industrial research organisations and industry in providing a diversity of experiences and qualifications to prepare our very highly qualified manpower for their place in a technological society.

- *What division of labour do we need to carry out the research mission at its most vital?* How many research leaders, how many dedicated research officers who can undertake the vital underpinning effort in research? What professional development should be provided? And finally, how many should we encourage to believe that they have a long-term future in research or teaching?

I doubt that the traditional academic career – with its combination of research, scholarship and undergraduate and postgraduate teaching – will last very much longer, given the increasingly specialist demands of the various missions of universities. Nor may it long be possible for the training of academic staff to be conducted in quite the amateur way it is now. Harsh words: but if one looks at the history of the PhD – the cornerstone of our development of the academic workforce – we see complaints throughout that it is inadequate even as a preparation for teaching and research. This is the degree which we then wish to promote to industry and commerce as a desirable qualification – when it does not even properly meet universities' own demands. We have to recognise that careers are more flexible nowadays. People can expect to have many different roles, and be called upon to contribute different skills throughout the course of their working lives, whatever sectors they work in. So the initial training has to be robust and strong on the core skills, as well as conveying specialist knowledge. In addition to specialist training, all postgraduate students should be given an appreciation of the business or commercial environment, should experience working in a team, and should have the opportunity to develop their presentational skills.

A much more measured view needs to be taken of the volume of people to be trained to post-doctoral levels. Universities will need to attend to their specialist development and to review with the individual, on a continuing basis, their long-term career prospects, whether within or without the Science Base and higher education. In our White Paper Advice, we again emphasised the need for universities, Research Councils and industry to work together to provide selectively deployed, long-term support, so that more coherent research careers can be made available for those with the necessary talent and motivation. Such partnerships should not detract from a university's central role as the employer of the research workforce, but there should be a dialogue between providers and purchasers of contract research to work towards employment conditions which will make the most of human resources. I endorse the suggestion made in the recent Committee of Vice Chancellors and Principals' (CVCP) document, *Promoting People,* that the introduction of a professional human resource management capacity in universities would be most advantageous, though we went further in our White Paper Advice in defining what is needed.

One of the first tasks I identified for senior university management was to define the particular mission, or niche, of their institution. I have also argued that attention needs to be given to the organisational structure of the university, if the research mission is to be pursued effectively, so that the critical mass of research effort and interdisciplinarity can be maintained. I have argued that personnel policies will also have to be tailored to recruit, train and retain those most appropriate to particular missions.

When I look back, as I have today, what strikes me is how peculiar to a particular time and place, is the model of the university that is so often defended in academic circles – a model which combines basic research and teaching at undergraduate and postgraduate levels. George Bugliarello, President of the Brooklyn Polytechnic University in the US, wrote something recently that gave me pause:

> The university has become adept at survival, to the point that it is not always clear whether the great range of activities in which universities are engaged today represents a deep ideological commitment or simply a manifestation of the need to survive.

He concludes that the time has come to assess what universities can and cannot do. Some major companies have survived adverse economic climates by diversifying their activities and keeping a toe in many different markets, both globally and by sector. Many others have collapsed through similar strategies. Diversification strains the capital resources of the company, severely tests the skills base of its personnel and challenges its management abilities to absorb the characteristics of a wide variety of markets. Many universities from the old university sector no doubt feel more comfortable at present with a diversified portfolio of activities. I am not so sure that with a sharper market in the future they may not find themselves overstretched – in terms of people, capital and management. An undergraduate teaching mission, a graduate or basic research mission, a technological mission: all of these are honourable callings – but I am not sure that you can be all things to all markets.

I want to end on a positive note. While earning your bread and butter by meeting the needs of sometimes rather difficult customers is not an easy task, I predict that universities are going to find that there is a pretty healthy market for what they are able to provide. Although funding from public sources in support of basic investigation to promote the advancement of knowledge is likely to be increasingly selectively deployed, the universities will, I believe, continue to attract the major part of that resource. Meanwhile, the sharpening competitive world of industry – with increasingly global markets – will mean that industries, such as pharmaceuticals or communications, will have to focus their own internal research and development efforts on bringing goods to the market. Hence, they will be even more enthusiastic purchasers of the kinds of flexibly-managed, wide-ranging, long-term research that universities can provide. Just as important, there will also be roles in disseminating technologies, especially to smaller companies – possibly through spin-offs from universities' own commercial arms – to say nothing of the growing demand, from an increasingly well educated population, for up-dating in the latest advances in science and technology.

So, potentially, we have a success story on our hands. The scientist and philosopher Francis Bacon once wrote: 'Hope is a good breakfast, but a bad supper'. But I think we do not have to be so pessimistic that the picture I paint of the future of universities is one of hopes alone. Just as universities have had a long and glorious past from Italy in the twelfth century, so they have the potential for an exciting and important future as a cornerstone of the modern economy. To quote from Bacon's *New Atlantis*:

> Among all the benefits that could be conferred among mankind, I found none so great as the discovery of new arts, endowments and commodities for the betterment of man's life.

Universities can truly be said to be among the chief providers of those arts, endowments and commodities in the modern world and, with imagination and resolve, they are well placed to continue in that role well into the future.

Discussion

Rodney Tulloch (Academic Secretary, Oxford Brookes University): We have just been advised of the dangers of trying to maintain diversity in hard times, and the American model, where institutions are increasingly concentrating either on research or on the teaching of undergraduates, has been cited with approval. In our own universities we are all having to decide whether to use resources to encourage what seem to us to be our strong research areas, or to infuse a research ethos into those areas which are not necessarily currently strong, and where we have, up till now, thought of research as supporting the undergraduate function and the development of the staff. Do you envisage large areas in higher education where staff will merely teach and do you see any danger that these people will suffer by being, in effect, cut off from researching?

Sir David: I am one of those who take the view that it is an obligation of all university academics to be deeply involved in scholarship which underpins their role in both teaching and research. The problem is that engaging in research at the highest level is becoming a highly competitive, international, full-time occupation, in which the competition is provided not only by people organised in full-time research units in other universities around the world, but also those working in Max Planck Institutes, for example, in countries where research is organised somewhat differently. So the question is, what sort of contribution can the part-time research worker/lecturer make in this highly competitive world? We all know that there have been examples, in the past, of people who are able to do a job while, at the same time, thinking about science and making revolutionary advances. Einstein is such an example. But that is getting to be increasingly difficult. I think we need, in this country, to get ourselves organised in universities in a somewhat more professional way.

Sir Terence Beckett (Chairman of Council, University of Essex): In discussing the management of research activities you referred to presentational skills and team working. It is my perception, having had a foot in both industry and the academic world, that one of our principal problems in the university sector today is a lack of professional management in the way research resources are handled. I am not talking just of the superstructure of the university: I am talking about the actual managerial content in each project team, and the fact that, in many cases, very little preparation is given to the people in that team. They find it out by accident and they look upon it as incidental to their main activity. Whereas, if we are going to use research resources to best effect, it needs some additional skills – for example, proper financial analysis, project management skills, and a professional attitude to the shortage of resources. There is far too much belly-aching generally in the university sector about the inadequacy of funding for this, that or the other. Those of us in industry know that we never have enough resources to do everything we want. Do you think there is any way that we could really produce a sea-change in the culture which would enable us to manage those resources better than we do today? How can we sharpen up the managerial approach?

Sir David: At the risk of being too provocative, I would say that in the research community management is a dirty word – and, surprisingly, it is considered a very unfortunate word even by some people who have most successfully managed quite large research enterprises. There is something about the ethos which does not associate with management. And that is a great pity. But it is something that is changing. During the 1960s and 70s, a view grew up in the university research community that each individual lecturer/professor needed to have his own research grant, and a student or two or a post-doc, to do his own thing. That meant that the management was down at a very low level of resource and, perhaps, did not seem terribly important. That is, in fact, is a rather old model. The effort of the Cavendish laboratory under Rutherford was all focused on his research programme, and he managed it all. You can read accounts of his regular morning meetings, hearing what the results were, working out what the resources were going to be, and so on. It was a heavily managed enterprise. Similarly with Robinson in Oxford, and Todd in Cambridge. There is a strong tradition of managing university research teams and managing them rather effectively in terms of the results they have produced. I think we need to see something of a return to that philosophy.

Alan Rudge (Managing Director, Development and Procurement, BT plc): In setting up major initiatives with universities one of the things we drove for was a more businesslike interface. I believe very strongly that science and engineering graduates need to know about time, money and people, as well as technology. The product management aspect of delivering a result from a research or development project is absolutely key. We expect university collaborators to demonstrate that they have reasonable project management capabilities and can manage their programme. That is part of the selection process. We choose groups that have the scientific and engineering capabilities and the elements of project management which enable them to deliver. We can help to achieve cultural change by using money as the offering that we make in return for more discipline from the university. The quality of the science does not suffer at all from having a more disciplined approach.

Professor Desmond Nuttall (Institute of Education, University of London): I think there is a new climate of willingness to take on the managerial aspects of research, and staff development programmes encourage us to be more managerial and think about these aspects of project management. I am a social scientist in a field where we have fewer post-doctoral fellowships than is customary in the natural sciences. We have very many contract researchers and it is our experience that the length of contract is becoming shorter and shorter. Many contract workers are part-timers and with very uncertain career prospects. You referred to our responsibilities to look after their creativity, but I wonder if you could help us with ideas about the personal and career development of so many people in such a precarious position.

Sir David: That raises a topic of major importance. I wonder, first, why you insist on having all these people associated with you, rather than indicating that there is no long-term future for them in the university system and telling them to find something else to do. That is the reality of it most of the time. For those who do find a place in the system there is strong case – just as with graduate students – for steering them towards a professional qualification which will be useful to them. University supervisors ought to be thinking whether the experience post-doctoral workers and contract research workers are getting is adding to their professional development and whether it is opening up new job opportunities, not simply in the university system, but in the wider world. I think universities have been acting – and largely are acting – very irresponsibly about this cadre of people.

Professor Nuttall: We do this research because researchers in local authorities and other organisations have been losing their jobs and there are masses of customers wanting us to do small-scale studies for them. The market for research is there and customers are keen for us to do it.

Sir David: Then you should set up a proper organisation, with properly organised professional staff, to respond to this contract research need.

Alan Rudge: I support that totally. The idea that because you are doing project work you can only employ people for the length of the project is totally amateur. Many organisations have to deal with short-term projects but can run their people on long-term staff contracts. If you cannot do that then there is something wrong with either the market or the organisation.

Professor David Harrison (Chairman, Committee of Vice-Chancellors and Principals): As an engineer I seem to be the first person to point out that you did present the totality of your address without mentioning research in the humanities or the social sciences. You may wish to comment on that. I should also like to pick up the point about the improvement in the management of research resources in more recent years. We must always remember the output of research in relation to the resources that are put in, and we do need to make international comparisons with Germany, Japan or the United States. On an output basis I rather think that British science, engineering, social science and the humanities would not do too badly.

Sir David: The ABRC is responsible for advice on the funding of the social sciences through the Economic and Social Research Council, and I would have done well to make an explicit mention of them. I set great importance on the development of the social sciences and their improved interaction with the natural sciences and engineering. In saying that I do not wish to imply that the difficulty arises on the side of the social sciences – there is a two-way problem of communication. The social science activity which is funded through the Research Council at the level of about £40m – a great deal more money comes in from other contractors and from the university block grant – is a very important element in our university research system. It is, perhaps, a little different from research in the natural sciences. Although there are social science projects such as the rather large project at the University of Essex for example, which requires long-term funding and quite a large team, there is still rather more scope for the individual research worker in the social sciences. That is probably even more true of the humanities. It was perhaps natural that I should overlook the humanities since there is not yet a humanities research council. I would very much like to see the humanities brought into the research council picture in one way or another.

Quentin Thompson (Coopers & Lybrand): You drew back from suggesting that all the dual support funds for research should be allocated on a project basis because of the uncertainties that such a major shift would give rise to in universities in the planning of their research. How long do you think universities need to settle down to the new method of research funding, before the remaining element of funding can be shifted and the salaries of academic staff engaged on research can be allocated on the same basis?

Sir David: It was a reasonable assumption from what I said that I thought this final transfer would be a good idea, but I am not absolutely convinced. There are two alternatives. One is the Funding Council block grant route, with somewhat improved accountability. The other is to make the full transfer, so that not only the funding of the marginal costs of projects but also of university salaries and the upkeep of premises becomes more market-oriented. That is not that far from the current American system, which many of us will know also causes difficulty; it will be a very radical shift in this country and I do not know either whether we shall be ready for it or whether we ought to do so.

Professor Richard Jones (Pro-Vice-Chancellor, University of East Anglia): You referred to the origin of public funding of research as being the initiation of technology transfer. You made a very clear distinction between mere market research and applied research. Speaking as a chemist, I come from an area in which we are not that bad at transferring technology, and the chemical industry clearly recognises that. One end of our fairly continuous spectrum is near-market research which it is their business to fund. At the other end is the seed-corn research, and that is appropriately public-funded. The chemical industry has quite a good record of putting money into higher education institutions in the rather grey area in between, of more speculative research. It is the very close contact that this generates between academics and industrialists which is part of the reason that the chemical industry and the pharmaceutical industry, in particular, is as excellent as it is. Can you see ways in which we can improve technology transfer throughout industry as a whole?

Sir David: I rather object to the phrase 'technology transfer' although it has very wide currency because, in a sense, it enshrines the linear model of the interaction between basic science and industry – the proposition that ideas emerge in basic science, go through some process of development through applied research, are taken up by industry and, in the end, emerge as a new product or process. The real world is much more complicated and much more interactive than that. We need an expression which shows that our target is to get as good interaction between all sectors of industry and the academic community as we have between the chemical and pharmaceutical industries and their part of the academic community. Essentially it is a problem of two-way or several-way communication, which we need to promote, and I think it boils down to saying what we need to do is increase the confidence of people on both sides of industry and academia in talking to one another.

Tom Kelly (Scottish Office): I see a trend at the moment – and my own department is a good example – of large purses of money being distributed among greater numbers of purse-holders, sometimes with rather different views about how the money should be used. Do you think the research community should resist that trend in the public services or should simply learn to live with it?

Sir David: In general, I think there is much to be said for diverse sources of funding, so that the decision-making does not simply lie with one or two people. But since the division of the funding councils between the three countries has not actually increased the sources of funding for different universities, they simply have different people to go to in terms of their block grants. If you like to entertain the thought that an English university could apply to you for funding, I think that could be rather a good idea. But I doubt if you will do that.

Tom Kelly: The point is not so much just about the territorial split, but the tendency to delegate budgets. For instance we have heard from universities of concerns about big budgets being passed, say, to hospital trusts and other organisations at a lower level, so that instead of facing one purse-holder for a large budget, universities may find a large number of purse-holders with relatively small budgets.

Sir David: The problem with medical education and medical research is actually quite a difficult one. I do think, however, that the fact that universities no longer have to deal with a single block grant, but with a multiplicity of funders who are after different products, does increase their managerial task and the need for their managerial capability.

Alan Rudge: I think the simple principle that should be applied wherever possible is that the funding should be with the customer who receives the output. I think that is a more effective way of drawing out the right outputs from the research activity.

Barry Seward-Thompson (Consultant, Open Minds): In most human activities we develop excellence both by helping people to a greater understanding and by giving them very practical challenges. For centuries the universities have developed learning and creativity in their students by taking people who already show unconscious ability to learn and create, and firing practical challenges at them. But there is no help at all in the understanding of a student's personal learning and creative processes. How much more could be achieved in terms of effectiveness if universities started to develop actively people's understanding of their personal learning and creative capability by sharing some of the very good work that has been done to understand how people tick, and in this way to enable them to control and extend their capabilities so as to enhance the quantity, quality and relevance of their attainment?

Sir David: That touches on the relationship between the natural sciences and the social sciences. There is a divide there which we desperately need to bridge, not only in university teaching and learning but also in industry and elsewhere. The traditional university way of dealing with postgraduates – and even, in some universities, with undergraduates, through the tutorial system – is essentially an apprenticeship system. Research leaders tend to produce students in their own image and, in the process, they certainly begin by demonstrating to students how to handle particular problems, and what skills they need to acquire. They then go on to challenge them: first, with modest original tasks and, finally, with a research problem of their own. That tradition still operates widely although, in the fully-fledged graduate school system, the process is engaged in rather more collectively than individually. I do not know of anyone who has attempted to understand, in detail, what the aptitudes of students are, and I will say, provocatively, that I think academics are too prone simply to see their graduate students and post-doctoral assistants simply as a useful pair of hands. They carry them forward on a wave of enthusiasm that they will become great research workers, whereas most of them are unlikely to do so.

Professor Ken Gregory (Goldsmith's College, University of London): You touched on the need to think in terms of the numbers of post-graduate students that are required in training, including PhDs. Is there a potential danger that if one looks at the numbers required, inevitably one requires less than are produced at the present time, and that this country may be disadvantaged in the next century compared with others? I wonder if we need to think rather more flexibly about postgraduate training, and whether we need to try not only to project numbers but also to project different types of training as well.

Sir David: I would not want to leave you with the impression that I am suggesting that we need to go in for rigorous manpower planning of the style of the 1950s. I do not think anybody would be promoting that. But the PhD problem is really quite a compli-cated one; we support quite a lot of people and the motivation for doing so is at least twofold. We provide support because we need highly skilled scientists, engineers, social scientists, and students of the humanities, but also because postgraduates are perceived to be an essential part of research activity. In some branches of the natural sciences – chemistry, for example -the view is that the research is done by graduate students, and their supervisors simply tell them what they want done. That means that they are not that interested in where the trained product might eventually go, although the fact is that chemical industry is interested not only in the training of those whom it recruits but also in their research con-tribution – and that is true in a good many areas of research activity. So it is a bit complicated.

  We need to recognise that we tend to use these people for our own academic purposes – for academic research with a view to academic employment – although by far the greater number of them are going to do something else. We need to worry a great deal about what is the appropriate higher education training to give graduate students who are not destined for work in higher education. This brings me back to the American model. I am well aware that American first degrees tend to be at a lower level, and less specialised

– though students do tend to major in a special topic at the end of their fourth year. However, at the end of graduate school with further courses and then a period of research, the American post-doctoral students are in no way inferior to their English equivalent, and are in many ways superior, particularly in their willingness to stand up and talk, to be criticised openly, and so on. I do think we have something to learn from all of that, and we are not being very quick in doing so.

4

University 2050: The Organisation of Creativity and Innovation

Professor Hans Van Ginkel, Rector Magnificus,
Utrecht University

Between Jules Verne and Dennis L Meadows

Making predictions about the future, however tempting, is fraught with risk. Nevertheless, I am very honoured by the invitation to share some thoughts on the theme of universities and university-systems as they might evolve well into the twenty-first century. It is an important subject, yet all too often it is pushed aside by everyday issues, even within universities themselves.

My chosen title is deliberately ambiguous; *dubbel* we would say in our language. It could be no more than a simple question: how will creativity and innovation be organised in the twenty-first century? The meaning changes, however, as soon as we accentuate the article. Will universities in the next millennium still be **the** organisations *par excellence* of creativity and innovation?

The future is a challenge at a time when we are still trying to adjust to the present decade. We only just manage to take an overall view of what is going to happen in the rather near future. How will the Memorandum on Higher Education in the European Community finally work out? Or the Maastricht Treaty and the Edinburgh agreement? What will be the influence of the rise of a new political generation around the Clinton-Gore team? And what will developments in Eastern Europe bring in the coming years now that the honeymoon is definitely over? What, then, can be said about the future in the longer term, some fifty to a hundred years from now?

There are some interesting views of universities in the coming century. I am thinking here of those presented at a symposium organised in honour of the hundredth anniversary of the founding of the University of Chicago, or Jacques Lesourne's article *The Future of Industrial Societies and Higher Education*. But even these are only directed at the first period of the next century. I intend to take a longer view of the university in the twenty-first century and shall therefore attempt to adjust my crystal ball towards the middle of the next century, the year 2050 – more than a complete Kondratieff wave away.

Predicting the future creates a definite tension between the layman and the academic. Looking into the future is not only everyone's favourite pastime, but also one of the most critical elements in scholarship and science. But are we looking to the future as depicted through the imagination of Jules Verne, or as presented in Dennis L Meadows' scenario *The Limits to Growth*, better known as the Report of The Club of Rome? I wish to explore the future by focusing on two dominant processes, the up-scaling of society and the development of a knowledge-intensive society. These two processes have been going on for a long time. Increasingly, however, their effects and consequences will be crucial for the future of both society and the universities.

The University Today

Because of the profound changes now affecting our world, particularly western industrialised society, universities have attracted ever more attention. This has happened for both economic and social reasons. The relationship between university and society has become much more direct during the last few decades. Some recently developed tasks, particularly on the economic front, have become more explicit and must be combined with existing, more traditional functions. Some people, including the American academic Etzkowitz, are even talking of an academic revolution such as the one that occurred at the beginning of the last century when – in the Humboldtian tradition – research was added to the tasks of universities.

After a long period of relative calm, universities have become the focus of a broad social and international debate about the tasks of a university and the way in which it fulfils and should fulfil these tasks. While there is some suggestion of high expectations, there has also been strong criticism both of the attitude of universities and the way they carry out their tasks. The European Community

Memorandum, the Valade Report carried out by the French government in 1987, or the 1991 White Paper presented here in the UK, are just some of the many examples.

Universities have also been actively involving themselves in the debate surrounding the question of quality and renewal. I am thinking especially of the debates organised by the Standing Conference of Rectors, Presidents and Vice-Chancellors of the European Universities (CRE) for the 1991 bi-annual conferences in St Petersburg and my own university in Utrecht. This question of quality and renewal has inspired many others, such as Jaroslav Pelikan in his recent re-examination of Newman's *The Idea of a University*. Universities have always stressed the considerable social significance of university values. The signing of the Magna Carta of European Universities in Bologna in 1991 during the 900th anniversary celebrations of the university there, was an impressive way for 282 universities to do this.

There is no such thing as a precise definition of the concept of a university, yet we are agreed about the people who together make up the university; people who are creative, capable, critical and pro-fessional. What matters is the form and framework in which we can allow creativity and innovative power to reach their full potential. We will call this form and framework a university even if it may look very different in 2050 from the university we know today. And I want to approach the future of universities from the premise that there has always been scholarship. The Alexandria library, Plato's Academy, the monastic schools, and not least the medressa (mosque universities) in Arab countries were all predecessors of the university. This is no coincidence. It simply implies deeply rooted qualities in our civilisation. It gives me confidence that there will always be science and scientists, scholarship and scholars.

My frame of reference for looking at the future is based on the idea that what a university will be like in 2050 will depend to a large extent on how society looks then, both at an economic level and in socio-political terms. This is hard to predict and still hangs on the question of whether George Orwell's pessimistic vision of 1984 will yet turn out to be our fate, or whether Francis Fukuyama's optimism will triumph and we shall live in a stable world society of free citizens, as recently described in his valuable book *The End of History and the Last Man*.

Future Scenarios

When one thinks of the future of our civilisation, one strives to imagine as concrete a picture as possible. Orwell and Fukuyama appeal to the imagination for that reason alone. Such visions, however, tend to ignore the undercurrents that determine the level of civilisation. And I would like to say something about that, because we should not lose sight of the fact that the present world population is about five billion strong. In 1950 there were only two and a half billion people, and we expect the present population to double before 2050.

During the last year, the Central Planning Office of the Netherlands produced a long-term scenario for the world economy, *Scanning the Future*. This was a very ambitious, yet very serious publication, if I may cite the assessment of *Foreign Affairs*. Four scenarios were presented for the development of the world economy during the next twenty five years: Global Shift; European Renaissance; Global Crisis; and Balanced Growth.

Balanced Growth is the optimistic scenario, because it predicts economic growth at roughly three percent a year for all regions under environmentally acceptable conditions, which means that sustainable development could be guaranteed. To achieve this, however, we require determined democratic political leadership. In Global Crisis, on the other hand, everything goes wrong and we end up with a form of ecological crisis with very uncertain prospects. Global Shift and European Renaissance are primarily descriptions of events at regional levels, describing the possible development of the Pacific Rim as compared with Europe and the effects of this on other parts of the world.

I do not wish to talk about what might be the most likely scenario, because it is still unclear what the effects might be of, for instance, the dehydration resulting from large-scale ground water extraction in areas like the western United States. Anyone who has seen Dennis L Meadows' 1991 scenario *Beyond Limits*, knows that there are many factors that can turn the future one way or another.

I mention these scenarios in order to indicate that even within a small number of options there are already many and very different developments to analyse. But, one thing is clear to me. There will always be science and scholarship and hence scientists and scholars.

Even if we return to the Middle Ages – which, incidentally, is not my assumption – there will be scholarship. There will be a new Bede and a new Erasmus. I am not trying to say that history will repeat itself, but that even if almost everything is destroyed, even if Big Brother rules, then human curiosity will continue to ask questions and look around for solutions. That curiosity is the basis of all scholarship, the beginning of knowledge.

I should now like to concentrate on the two processes already mentioned which, to my mind, have been of crucial importance to the continuing development of both society and the university:

- the *upscaling of society*, that is, the combination of increases in scale with simultaneous narrowing of the processes of society – something akin to playing football in a higher division. In the end, there is only one division in the Honours League; even reserves are playing at the international level.

- the development of an *intensity of knowledge* in our society and therefore in our scholarship – in particular, the role of technological developments in furthering scholarship and passing it on.

Upscaling and Specialisation

In his magnificent work, *La Méditerranée et Le Monde à L'Epoque de Philippe II*, the historian Fernand Braudel is one of the first to pay specific attention to 'the measure of the century'. All sorts of points, such as the size of the world's population, or the time it took to send a letter, are described in order to give a picture of both the economic level and the general unity of the world. For instance, it used to take several weeks to send a letter from London to Venice. Braudel's pupil, Immanuel Wallerstein, has gone a few stages further, and described the development of the world economy and the associated integration of the world:

In the late fifteenth and early sixteenth century, there came into existence what we call a European world-economy… It is a world system, not because it encompasses the whole world, but because it is larger than any juridically-defined political unit. And it is a world-economy because the basic linkage between the parts of the system is economic.

Since then, what Wallerstein calls an 'ongoing process' has led to a system that extends geographically over the whole world. A number of different levels of intensity exist. The pulse is therefore much faster in London at 51 degrees North (and 10 minutes West), than in London at 2 degrees North, 157 degrees West. The heart also beats noticeably faster in Utrecht at 52 degrees North and 5 degrees East than in Utrecht at 27 degrees South and 30 degrees East. In short, London on Christmas Island, which is now called Kiritimati, and Utrecht on the slopes of Thabakulu in South Africa along with Viljoenpost and Grootspruit, are part of the world economy, but move at a rather slower pace. This also happens in Europe, as can be witnessed by the discussion about a two-speed Europe. Gorbachev expressed his desire for Greater Russia to achieve access to the world economy in much the same terms. And it is no different for universities.

The knowledge intensity at world economic level is enormous. Universities cannot be compared to the various stock exchanges, where traders deal with the whole world, using many telephones at the same time, but science and scholarship do certainly function at that world level. E-mail, television, fax machines and aviation, have caused the world to shrink. The weeks that were required centuries ago to pass a message between London and Venice have been replaced by seconds. At the same time the number of messages has multiplied beyond all recognition.

Leading academics have always pushed back frontiers, not only by expanding the limits of human knowledge and ability, but also by continuously bridging political and geographical borders. As increases in scale and globalisation progress further, so universities and research institutes are working together more and more on a much broader range of activities. This naturally leads to further fine-tuning and profiling of separate universities. The cost of ground-breaking research naturally encourages this tendency.

Networking

Globalisation will progress further. The way in which international contact will develop is, however, a moot point. Opportunities for communication are multiplying at a sensational rate. We will still prefer to talk face-to-face rather than on the telephone, especially when talking to someone who comes from another culture. However, the stock market traders I have already evoked gave this up a long time ago, and many academics are already in everyday contact with colleagues around the world, without ever having seen them. E-mail allows them to stay in better contact with Chris Barber in Australia or Pedro Gonzalvez in Venezuela than with another academic in the same building, whose hair colour they know, but nothing about his research, unless it is directly related to their own. That this leads to deepening individualisation among academics should be obvious.

It seems to me that globalisation in the western hemisphere will lead to greater unity whatever happens. But this will not be the unity envisaged by Napoleon two centuries ago, with the same laws and the same straight roads stretching right across Europe. It will be, and indeed ought to be, a unity in diversity, based on the principles of subsidiarity. It will also apply to universities in a big way. They have a tradition of diversity stretching back to their origins, as is so clearly outlined in the excellent first volume of *A History of the University in Europe*, which appeared recently under the auspices of the CRE. Universities will become increasingly inter-linked and bound to one another, while also identifying themselves as distinct from each other. The anomaly of the 'national university', as it existed between the middle of the nineteenth century up to the middle of the twentieth century, can now only be alluded to in the past tense, just as the nation state seems to have been merely a ripple in the current of history.

The network one belongs to will become increasingly important, since it will contribute directly to the attractiveness of a university and its international position. It is possible that international networks will form the basis of the university in the future. However, I do not think it will be long before the larger universities have set up institutes abroad, and we can see this in a number of institutions in the UK already. The university will become an international business, in every sense. Many existing universities will come under the hammer during the process, but that is old news. Some of the oldest universities affected are Reggio, Vicenza, Palencia, Arezzo and, in my own country Harderwijk where Linnaeus once gained his doctorate. The institute university is evolving all the time.

The Knowledge-Intensive Society

The increasing knowledge-intensiveness of society and science does not require much elucidation. Roughly speaking, it means that:

- more and more knowledge will be produced: estimates say the amount of knowledge can now double every five years;

- the shelf-life of knowledge will decline rapidly. American publications cited in the patent rolls in 1975 were eight years old on average, but only six and a half years old on average ten years later;

- average levels of education will rise.

The whole concept of education will shift as a result of this knowledge intensification, and this will have a fundamental influence on universities. The increasing importance of learning throughout the course of one's working life will play an important role. This is currently a strong focus of interest, and with good reason. Countless conferences bear witness to it, and it is also high on the political agenda of Clinton's administration.

Academia is gaining a progressively stronger influence on society. The knowledge-intensive economy is replacing the work-intensive economy and the capital-intensive economy. The Dutch government is one of those to have already stressed the importance of academia to society: 'Today we are witnessing waves of important discoveries. They are so significant that some people even compare them to those of the first industrial revolution.' This influence of scholarship on civilisation is expressed very recognisably in the influence of technology on civilisation. The 1990 report of the EC Advisory Committee on Industrial Research and Development (IRDAC), *Skill Shortages in Europe*, goes into this in great detail. Many other writers have also stressed this, including Kenneth Keller, who describes the influence of technological development on United States foreign policy.

What has also increasingly become knowledge-intensive is the duo of science and scholarship themselves. The knowledge-intensification of scholarship pervades all stages of the academic process.

Managing knowledge, processing other people's research and staying abreast of developments elsewhere are all becoming more and more important. The profession of knowledge-broker will emerge. The whole infrastructure will change. One of the Clinton-Gore team's commitments is to the development of a national information structure. Europe will undoubtedly follow suit. Discussion has also started on how to transform a university library from functioning as a memory bank to functioning as an interactive partner in the thinking process. Knowledge engineering is on the rise.

The Power of Technology

The knowledge-intensification of science and scholarship will increase technology's capacity to distribute and develop knowledge. Without wishing to become involved in any Azimov-type speculation here, it would not appear to be an unreasonable claim that during the next fifty years unbelievable developments in the area of artificial intelligence technology will take place. We should certainly not under-estimate the consequences of this for both scholarship and society. Much depends, therefore, on how quickly we can achieve a better understanding of what intelligence actually is. I would, however, not wish to enter into this classic philosophical debate. I shall therefore restrict myself to making a few general points:

- It is important to remember that the future does not begin at any specific moment. There are processes and developments. Think of the increasingly technological society in which we live. The first PCs were brought onto the market by Apple only in the late 1970s. Now we could not live without them. If computers were suddenly made illegal, civilisation would collapse in a single day.

- Raymond Kurzweil, an MIT employee, has written a thoroughly admirable book *Intelligent Machines*, to which Marvin Minsky, Daniel C Dennett and Douglas R Hofstadter also contributed. Kurzweil piles prediction upon prediction. He expects that

  – by the turn of the century there will be 'telephones answered by an intelligent answering machine' and 'speech-to-text machines which translate speech into a visual context for the deaf.' His vision of a future in which 'computers dominate the educational environment, courseware is intelligent enough to understand and correct the inaccuracies in the conceptual model of the student' is also an interesting prospect.

– in the long run, between 2020 and 2070, there will be a truly intelligent machine. In technical jargon, this is a machine which passes the Turing test, and therefore achieves the level of human intelligence.

• Thinking machines no longer belong to the realm of the imagination. In fact we see them around us already. Supercomputers scan and analyse the heavens and medical research is no longer conceivable without high-tech apparatus. Interactive video-disks and other educational tools are being rapidly developed. Artificial intelligence is on the rise, just like virtual reality. It is likely that in a few decades we will have artificial intelligence that does not only conduct a large amount of independent research, but also simultaneously decides what should be done with the results – that both collects and distributes knowledge independently.

• Ultimately, the most important factors in the future of the university are flows of knowledge, which develop themselves and interlock – in other words, self-developing knowledge systems. It is more than ten years since Patrick Winston, also from MIT, proclaimed that the idea that you can never obtain from a machine more than you put into it seems to have been superseded.

The prospect of self-developing knowledge systems might be a little frightening, and I have not even begun to talk about biological knowledge systems. Nonetheless, this is not a simple question of whether man will be outstripped by machines. Human knowledge and insight will develop further during the coming decades. It is not really a case of thinking in terms of winners and losers. People will concentrate more on directing and mastering the flows of knowledge. This will require techniques beyond anything we now know, far more complex than the knowledge engineering I have just mentioned.

The University of the Future

So far, I have been trying to come up with a picture of the society within which universities will operate. This society will obviously differ greatly from the current one. Or, to use the words of Robert Reich:

> We are living through a transformation that will rearrange the politics and economics of the coming century. There will be no national products or technologies, no national corporations, no national industries. There will no longer be national economies, at least as we have come to understand this concept. All who remain rooted within national borders are the people who comprise a nation.

Knowledge has come to dominate the economy more and more, and thus also regional developments. Reich adds to this that people are the least mobile factor in international traffic. Everything else is in motion, but people are bound to one place socially and economically. It is not easy to move billions of people around, so government policy will be directed to strengthening local economic capacities, which means, largely, education.

Knowledge is ultimately the most important raw material, and it is the only one which can be continuously enriched. It is the most important thing which man is capable of adding to nature. I should perhaps paraphrase Descartes' well-known saying here: 'we think, therefore we are'. It seems obvious, as Reich states, that the existing knowledge infrastructure, especially in Europe and North America, should form the basis of world-wide co-operation.

I have demonstrated so far that scholarship will always exist. I have also devoted time to two processes central to the development of society: upscaling and globalisation on the one hand and increasing knowledge-intensity in society and academia on the other.

This makes a strong case for high-level practice and passing on of science and scholarship, but should this necessarily take place in the university? This question is unavoidable once we start looking at the increasing co-operation between universities and society. Will the university, in the words of Professor Clark Kerr of the University of California, Berkeley, become an anachronism and will it be swallowed up by business and government? Will company training and company laboratories simply take over the role of the university?

This seems a serious prospect to me, but there are two things which persuade me that it is not what the future holds. First of all, an umbrella organisation will always be necessary to guide and combine flows of knowledge, a requirement which no company training scheme could fulfil. Secondly, it seems absolutely vital to me that knowledge retains its broad basis and that the preservation of scholarship and the generation of theory are guaranteed a permanent place. Science and scholarship will not be able to develop much further without them.

Nevertheless, great changes will inevitably come to pass:

- universities will concentrate very heavily on guiding and combining flows of knowledge;

- they will, consequently, develop their own research to a lesser extent; and

- a new concept of education will emerge; content will be more general and learning will be conducted throughout an individual's entire life.

This implies shifts in the nature of research, education and knowledge management. The diminished importance of research is a much older phenomenon than it might appear. Scientific discoveries and research have often come to fruition beyond the bounds of the university. Newton had his *annus mirabilis* before he was appointed professor in Cambridge in 1669. It was not until the last century that Humboldt's philosophy led the attempt to bring research within the bounds of the university. This was what Etzkowitz calls the First Academic Revolution. However, to take one example, this only happened to a limited extent in France, and a great deal of research in Germany was conducted outside universities in the Max Planck institutes. Nevertheless, universities have always played and will continue to play a crucial role in the organisation and development of scholarship and the training of scientists and scholars. They encompass a broad range of independent scientific developments and they educate new generations of scholars and scientists to make breakthroughs in research within, but very often outside, the universities.

The purpose of universities will come to be ever more bound up with the mastery and guidance of knowledge development. But is the university as supervisor such a peculiar concept now? Is the idea of knowledge management as the central distinguishing factor of the university of the future such a strange idea? I would say not. It fits in with the university's classical role of preserving existing knowledge and passing it on within a broad conception of academia: testing and improving the quality of knowledge; developing knowledge further; using combination and confrontation as tools. The classical role of the university is both to bring cohesion to scholarship and to stimulate creativity. This broad approach holds great potential for the university of the future, including the following examples:

- Many of the great breakthroughs have been made on the fringes of disciplines as they encounter influences from contact with other disciplines. Consider bio-physics for example, which has taken on the leading role which physics played during the first half of the century. 'As physics did at an earlier time, the bio-sciences emerge as important because of their technological potential', as Keller postulated.

- Different practical experiences and knowledge have to be brought under one roof somewhere. The British university – described so fascinatingly in Noel Annan's *Our Age* – where reading was once more important than publishing, no longer exists. But people still read things and remember them. It was and remains the university's task to transmit the past and to make it accessible.

Network or Barracks?

Will, then, the university of Big Brother's world look a great deal different from the one in the world of the free citizens of Fukuyama? Is the university of the future a barracks in which scholars and knowledge managers are barricaded against the world or confined in a kind of reservation? Or will the university of the future have no buildings at all, and simply consist of myriad international networks to which people are connected – a world-wide neurological system with a bulletin board at its heart?

As I see it, there are a number of reasons why universities will continue to have recognisable locations and space:

- There is a basic human need for meeting in the flesh and engaging in communal rituals. Direct debate is the finest servant to the stimulation of creativity and innovation. Academics and knowledge managers will certainly need to be in the same physical space when it comes to matters of policy and debates regarding the generation of general scientific and scholarly theory. This contributes to academic cohesion.

- In preserving academic cohesion, scholars will also play a role in the interaction between academia and society. This is another reason why universities will remain recognisable entities. An accountable administration is necessary if society is to maintain a grip on the university.

In other words, the university will always be somewhere. I cannot see scholars and knowledge managers shutting themselves away like Chinese mandarins. They will not be given the opportunity to do so. I regard this as a boon, since the genuinely innovative university will always be one which reacts to social developments and the demands made by society.

Until now I have been reflecting upon the nature of the university during the next century. However, this is all seen from a definitely western perspective, so I would like to say something about the university in developing countries. In general, the question arises as to whether developing countries will be able to keep up with upscaling or whether they will become the 'slums of the global village'. This is the central question in the recently published Dutch government policy paper, *A world of difference; a new framework for development co-operation in the 1990s*. In this White Paper the foundations are laid for the policy on development co-operation for the next decade. The Dutch government, among other initiatives, pleads in favour of developing higher education and research in developing countries themselves. Special attention is focused on supporting regional postgraduate institutes, for economic, political and social reasons. These regional institutes may be part of international networks. The EC Memorandum also advocates this course of action. My feeling is that the issue of the university in developing countries is rather more than an issue of solidarity. It is also a test of how well thought-out our policy towards our own universities is. One of the university's traditional tasks is to contribute to the international community in the cultural and social sense. If we forsake the universities outside our own western hemisphere, then we are also forsaking a classical task of the university.

The Organisation of Creativity and Innovation

This lecture has been a plea based partly on hope and partly on analysis of developments: hope regarding the general development of the world; hope that no catastrophes lie ahead and hope that current academic freedom can survive. The analysis has been based on two long-term processes: upscaling, which has been under way for centuries, but has now been caught up in an accelerating current of change; and the developing of a knowledge-intensive society, partly fed by unprecedented technological developments.

Together, this mixture of hope and analysis gives me cause to believe that the university will remain the centre of creativity and innovation well into the middle of the next century, and remain firmly fixed in the midst of society. This university will look rather different from the university we know today. It will be an international business in every sense. Knowledge management will occupy the centre stage. Countless flows of knowledge, most of which will operate independently, need to be guided and mastered. This cannot be seen as separate from preserving broadly-based science and scholarship and generating theory. But if all this is the case, what are the consequences for the near future? I see challenges on the horizon in many areas during the coming years. Before I conclude, I should like to mention a few:

- The process of organised internationalisation must be intensified at every level. I would ask for particular attention for universities in developing countries. Internationalisation must be expressed in choices made by a university concerning profile, joint ventures and selective networking.

- While the debate on the tasks of the university goes on and while notice is taken of society, innovation and creativity in the university must be strengthened.

- I am sure that quality assessment will occupy a progressively more central position in the day-to-day business of science and scholarship. But this can only be done in a responsible manner if a staged approach is adopted, with a great deal of flexibility at university level. This is why I applaud recent initiatives on the part of the CRE and the Liaison Committee to set up a number of pilot projects at the European level. This is quality control initiated on the university's own responsibility.

- And, last but not least, I would like to appeal for greater attention to cohesion in science and scholarship, also on the basis of social considerations. If the university of the future wants to preserve, develop and pass on knowledge, scholarship will require greater cohesion. This will mean that C.P. Snow's distinction between the humanities and natural sciences will become a thing of the past. The cry for this has already gone out in many quarters, both in the IRDAC report and from an expert no less than Frederico Major, director general of Unesco. I must admit, though, that both parties think the other needs to be convinced.

There is a future for universities. In principle, they can respond to it in two different ways. They can wait and see – as Einstein said 'I never think of the future, it comes soon enough' – since the future comes on its own, and without warning. Alternatively, they can attempt to shape developments, and I am in favour of this option. In that case, there are a great many problems to be overcome. For, to cite Niels Bohr: 'It is hard to predict – especially the future'. But let us start right away to work all together on this unpredictable future in an energetic and systematic way, taking into account all credible, sound foresight we can mobilise.

Discussion

Barry Seward-Thompson (Consultant, Open Minds): At the beginning of your lecture you asked whether universities will still be **the** organisations of creativity and innovation by the year 2050. There is a major assumption in that question to the effect that they are so today. I do not know about Utrecht, but I have quite a lot of experience of UK universities and, although some change is slowly happening now, I do not think one has to be too mischievous to argue that an eighteenth century academic would recognise the teaching methods, organisations and power structures in most UK universities today. I would argue that narrowly-defined, scholarship-based creativity and innovation tends to occur despite the system rather than because of it. Surely the challenge for universities, at least in the UK today, is not to remain, but actually to become, the organisations of creativity and innovation by the year 2050?

Professor van Ginkel: I have described elsewhere what is happening in Dutch universities in regard to fixed curricula, tests and examinations. In this situation, I sometimes doubt whether the best students can really develop creativity and innovation. Nevertheless, I think that universities – at least in my country – are, at the moment, in the best position to be organisations of creativity and innovation *par excellence*. At the moment there are no better ones, even though existing universities could be much improved. One of the major causes of failure is that universities, in the process of 'massification', have become too much like secondary schools in their programmes and in the behaviour not only of the staff but of the students. In many instances we have put too much focus on trying to include in the curriculum all the content and disciplines we think important. Very often there are many specialised scientists in a department or faculty and each of them wants to have a part of the curriculum. As a consequence we have packed our programmes with knowledge but there is not much to motivate or to educate students to pose the right questions and try to find the right solutions. I must stress that nowadays as knowledge doubles every five years and the shelf value of all knowledge is so short, the knowledge content of disciplines is probably less important for university programmes. You need some content in order to help the students to study a discipline or to learn from example. We should try to make programmes shorter and allow more time for research-style activity.

Professor Gareth Williams (Institute of Education, University of London): If we have the kind of scenario you are implicitly assuming, do we not run the risk of seeing the university, at least in the sense you mean it, and the knowledge possessors, getting further and further away from those who have less access to knowledge? If I had to summarise what has happened in the last hundred years it is that the gap between those with access to advanced knowledge and those without is getting wider and wider. I wonder if you have any views on whether there are certain dangers in that development if, indeed, it is a likely development?

Professor van Ginkel: When you say the gap between those who have access to knowledge and those who have not has increased over time, I think one must, at the same time, accept that at least in my country and more generally – I think Great Britain is fairly close to that too – 30% of the age group, climbing to 35%, is now attending some course in a higher education institution. That group really is increasing and, at the same time, the majority of institutions of higher education are committed to trying to contribute to the demand for knowledge. Many higher education institutions now have liaison officers to establish links with medium and small size firms, to contribute to developments in the region, and so forth. I am not really sure whether the gap has increased. But the system of higher education is changing all the time. In the past, when society was not as knowledge-intensive as it is now, there were programmes for only a few professions in the universities. The need for professional training on a fairly high level is increasing considerably and, for many professions nowadays, higher learning is an asset. Society has the choice whether to include all of those programmes in universities or to organise them outside.There has been discussion on binary systems. In southern Europe there are massive institutions where everything is brought together under the name *university*. In Great Britain, a good example was set when polytechnics were developed and, in fact, Germany, with the *Fachhochschulen*, and the Netherlands with the HBO sector have followed suit. But I am now confused because of what happened a few months ago in Britain.

What we must try to prevent is academic drift. When you look at an age group and try to bring the best 30% or 35% of the group into higher education, then clearly there will be differences in talent between the first 10% and the other 25% – or wherever you want to make the division. At the same time, the demands of society for trained people vary. Sometimes society needs really omni-valent, creative, abstract-thinking people educated through a rather general curriculum in whatever discipline and, on the other hand, it needs the really well trained, pragmatic, adjusted-to-the-job-market output of the higher learning and higher education institutions. In the Netherlands, we decided to keep the two lines distinct and here you have brought everything together.

Roderick Peyton (Buckinghamshire College of Higher Education): I am very interested in your stress on the knowledge-intensive society. Having worked with a number of European and American universities over the last twenty to twenty-five years I have been very struck by the difference in approach, between all the other countries and England, in their understanding of what they are trying to do in education. In Italy and Germany, for example, it seems to me that they are convinced that the purpose of education is to learn something, to take information and absorb it. The English view is quite the reverse: that you are actually trying to draw something out of people and to develop them. If there is a knowledge-intensive society with this extraordinary turnover of knowledge – rather like throwing away your computer, your hardware and software every two or three years – is it best to take the view that you are not going to learn the knowledge anyway and you might as well learn how to cope without it – which I would suggest is the English view – or is it better desperately to develop models for learning the knowledge and then chuck it out after five years and learn the next batch?

Professor van Ginkel: In general, in Continental Europe, the most important part of university studies has been what can you teach – what kind of information you transfer to the new generation. I stressed in my talk that I am not convinced that is the best approach – at least for the future. I am very much in favour of the general Anglo-Saxon – in particular the British – way of looking at education, as trying to extract things from people. I believe the stress should be on libraries that inform students, in an interactive way, about the things they need to know, instead of being mere storehouses of written knowledge. The stress should not be on big audiences and lectures but much more on working forums and programmes where students really learn to find solutions.

Professor A H Halsey: You have chosen to talk about the possibility of a mid-twenty-first century university which has the distinctive function of somehow being the vanguard – the articulator – of creativity and innovation. Your audience appears to be assuming that the best bet is to suggest that even in the middle of the twenty-first century most countries will still have a large, sieving, selecting operation to decide who can and who can not enter into the world of knowledge management and even what proportion of the population that should be. The recent history of the European universities is very much that. You are really telling us two quite contradictory things: on the one hand you do believe that the university will be there in the twenty-first century, but you are also saying on the other hand that, looking back, there is no evidence that the universities have ever had a monopoly of creativity and innovation. On the whole they have not. What they have done is to provide a sort of sanctuary for those who are interested in that kind of thing, and they have had a short period – very short actually – of being rather successful and dominant. You could, however, have argued in the opposite direction, following Ernest Gellner. The whole project is about incorporating the life of modern societies into a very much more complicated knowledge system than has ever been before. That is why Gellner says that it is not the policeman but the professor who is at the basis of the social order. But when it comes down to it a professor is really dispensable. You can take a businessman or a politician or a journalist and substitute him for the professor and nobody would particularly notice the difference. There might be one or two exceptions, specially gifted teachers, for example. But on the whole that is the way it is. There is a kind of substitutability, says Gellner, for this particular role. I think we could all agree that, accepting that the university has a monopoly of nothing, it is still very likely that unless we resort absolutely to barbarism there will still, in the middle of the twenty-first century, be a demand for creativity and innovation, but it might take any form. It might take a very large number of different forms in different countries.

Professor van Ginkel: In my lecture I did not make a choice at the end, deliberately, because I think the important thing is the first interpretation: that the universities should contribute to the *organisation* of creativity and innovation. They may not have a monopoly, but they can play a major role, more particularly in the development of each new generation, and in focusing on the importance of creativity and innovation instead of copying the behaviour of others. Probably the outcome could be that they are the organisations *par excellence*, but then they would have to improve quite a lot in comparison with what they are now. I did not really describe what universities would look like the next century. I only pointed at trends but I have the idea that there will be very strong networks. The nodes may be independent organisations or they may be offshoots of the original university – as is sometimes seen when British or American universities establish institutions on the continent. It will be different for different types of discipline.

I played down the importance of the university as an organisation with one location and strong walls around it, and I am much more in favour of a kind of network organisation. The identity is then in the organisation itself. But whatever form it takes it should at least contribute significantly to the development of creativity and innovation in the younger generation. That is really the major role of universities within the whole system of higher education. But that does not mean that they are the places from which the new break-throughs in research will always come.

Catherine Graham-Harrison (Paul Hamlyn Foundation):I think there may be some confusion in the argument. When you were talking about being perplexed at what has happened in the UK recently – with the former polytechnics joining the old universities – you seemed to identify the previous split as between the univer-sities with the creative and innovative and the polytechnics with the practical. You have talked also about the continuation of the devel-opment of an intellectual elite. Now 'elite' may mean 35% of the population. It may mean 50%. But, to me, it means a smaller number. You have talked a lot about structures and I have had less sense of the individuals within those structures – the young people coming through. Do you not think, in terms of the future of those young people in the twenty-first century, that they would be better served by the diminution of the split between the creative and innovative and the practical? It seems to me that some of the most powerful people in any generation have been those who have combined the two, as opposed to perpetuating what to me is a myth: that you are either creative or you are practical. The coming together of our old and new universities to me symbolises an important acceptance that the two would work better together instead of being artificially split for all time.

Professor van Ginkel: People differ in their degree of creativity and in their capacity for abstract thinking and practical work. But abstract thinking will always form part of the education of those being prepared at higher education level for the labour market. Probably the confusion has arisen because of the differences in the educational systems of Britain and the Netherlands. In Great Britain, polytechnics were designed, from the beginning, to be much closer to the universities than is the case in the Netherlands or Germany, for instance. In the Netherlands, secondary schools which give entrance to higher education are on two different levels. Those which give entrance to the universities – without examinations, which is sometimes a point that people in the universities complain about – are six-year secondary schools. Those which give entrance to the HBO institutions are five-year secondary schools. There is not only one year less at school, but progress in the five-year secondary schools is also slower. The entrance levels to the higher education system are, as a result, quite different. Therefore, at least in the Netherlands, there is more interest in keeping the two lines of education separate.

Nevertheless, there has always been the idea, in the Dutch system, that, in principle, all children are the same and they can all learn, although to different degrees and at different rates. So you have those who learn less well at a younger age who make up for it in the later stages, and so on. The system is built up in such a way that you can switch from one system to the other at any time. Going from the higher system to the lower generally gives you a major advantage. Going from the lower – in terms of intellectual work – to the higher system generally means you have to make up for one or two years more.

5
The University in the Community
Dr Anne Wright, Vice-Chancellor, University of Sunderland

Looking backwards, looking forwards

The twenty-first century is not so very far away. The first graduates of the new century will soon be moving on to GCSE programmes, and the first new entrants to twenty-first century higher education are now embarking on their first year of secondary schooling. So we can assume that we are almost there – that many of the educational initiatives now in place will see us into the millennium. But how millenarian are they? Is our vision for higher education millenarian enough? Are we to strike out for a new century – a new millennium – addressing a Brave New World, thunderstruck by the new landscape spread before us? Or, have we merely the down-side of apocalypse, the sense of an ending – that sense of an ending which is, typically, perceived as decline and suffused with nostalgia for a lost golden age?

Millenarianism seeps into all areas of activity, but education – and indeed higher education – is perhaps particularly susceptible. Education is, after all, concerned with shaping the future as much as it is concerned with handing on the past. And, if it has a central belief it must be in a future achieved through people – shaping the future through people. Higher education – the universities – exist to advance knowledge, and to advance knowledge through people. Universities are the guardians of the future. Yet universities also cherish the past, preserving and transmitting ancient wisdom, knowledge and culture. Janus-like – looking backwards, looking forwards – we are perhaps peculiarly subject to the apocalyptic sense of an ending.

Even when universities look to the future, we find ourselves poised between the short-term and the long-term – between study relevant to employment, and knowledge for its own sake. Yet, after all, that tension too is intrinsic to our role. Universities advance knowledge through people for the benefit of individuals and society. We can only fulfil that mission by a delicate and constantly re-adjudged balance: a balance between the short-term needs and demands of students and industry and the longer-term advancement of knowledge; and a balance between a view of a higher education system which is geared for employment and a commitment to academic freedom and autonomy. Universities may well be acting in the interests of society by insisting on the long-term; but we constantly need to check and challenge that – to maintain the balance.

Universities must be independent; but this does not mean standing apart from society or its immediate environment. I do not believe that universities exist to serve knowledge, which is an abstract, but to serve people in the real world. They are a part of a higher education system which represents a choice made by society to produce people who are confident, capable and qualified to fulfil themselves and to contribute, over a lifetime, to society and the economy. It follows that I see modern universities as substantially, perhaps even primarily, institutions of higher *education*, places for *learning*, and that I see the *teaching of students* as central to their role and purpose, alongside research and innovation.

The Framework and the Goal

We could say that universities have already been redefined, and that the framework and the goal for the new century are already in place. Two defining factors for universities in the twenty-first century are, first, the shaping of the new single university sector and, second, the goal that has been set of one in three young people entering higher education by the year 2,000.

There are other defining contexts which impinge on these two and which are also central – the national education and training targets for foundation learning and lifetime learning, for example, and the responsibility laid on the new Further Education sector to increase staying-on rates in full-time education at the age of 17. Others will come, for example, as GNVQs gets up a head of steam alongside NVQs.

The 1992 *Further and Higher Education Reform Act* redefined universities and gave a framework for higher education for the next century. The White Paper which set out the rationale for the new framework spoke of the need to build on the successes of recent years in extending participation in higher education, and described the distinction between universities and polytechnics as 'an obstacle to further progress'. The change of title for the former polytechnics is a clarification, a change of status, but not a change of mission or of function. In a sense, very little has changed – we have the same institutions doing, at present at any rate, the same things. A new environment and a new funding regime may of course introduce a new diversity within the single sector.

But the point I wish to make here is that the change of name and status can, in itself, be a key to further progress by enhancing capability and releasing energy in the system. The term 'university' now includes institutions which bring a particular tradition, born of their history and their success as polytechnics, to this new and diverse single sector.

For the first time in this country, our universities, taken as a whole, include a wide range of programmes of vocational higher education including many new fields. Our universities teach at all levels from HNC and HND through to PhD. Universities cater explicitly for a range of students including mature entrants, women returners and unemployed people. They offer flexible patterns of attendance – sandwich, part-time – and flexible programmes, through modularisation and credit accumulation. They have well-developed practices for workplace learning; for accreditation of prior learning (APL); for academic as well as vocational programmes based on learning outcomes or competencies; and for developing transferable skills as well as specialist knowledge. They have strong and sophisticated links with employers, developed from long years of experience and their roots in local industry, and now extended by a variety of partnership strategies. They have twenty-five years' experience of highly developed quality assurance systems. They combine a strong sense of community, from their development through the local authorities, with the equally robust entrepreneurship which has followed incorporation.

These are the strengths which the former polytechnics bring to the new single sector to complement the strengths of the tradi-

tional universities. The history and the achievements of the polytechnics are now part of the collective strength and capability of the
university sector.

One in Three

The second redefinition arises from the move to an entry ratio of
one in three by the year 2,000. This target recognises the need to build
a world-class, competitive economy and a strong, confident society
through a better educated and better trained workforce. It com-
plements the targeted increases in staying-on rates in post-16
full-time education and training. The increase to 30 per cent is a continuation of the expansion seen in recent years, but it is more than
merely a continuation of a trend.

The move to a high-volume higher education system marks what
will be a cultural change. By the middle of the next century, between
a third and a half of the entire population of working age will be
graduates of initial higher education. Many will have additional
experience of higher education during their careers, for development or retraining. A substantial proportion of the total population
will be students, parents, partners or children of students, or will
themselves be employed in higher education. Higher education, both
initial higher education and in-career higher education and training,
will be a normal expectation: life-long learners and life-long nation-
wide learning.

These two factors – the reshaping of the sector, and the expansion
to a high-volume higher education system – mean that universities
will have a heightened role in the community and a more visible
contribution to society and the economy.

I wish to focus on the role of universities in the community, and
my assumptions are these:

- that the role of universities in the community is rich, multi-faceted
  and, above all, interactive – an active resource and a generator for
  individual and economic development

- that the role is flexible and changing, just as universities can
  themselves be agents of change, and

- that the new framework and the goal taken together put a new emphasis on the role of the university in the community.

Universities in the Community: *UniverCities* and urban regeneration

Universities have always had a role to play in the community, from AD 674 when Bede and Benedict Biscop came to Sunderland – for as you may not know, the University of Sunderland is the oldest seat of learning and Benedict Biscop was its first vice-chancellor – to the foundation of Sheffield University by eager city fathers, keen that their city should not be without the benefits which they felt a university could bring. The role has been rethought: from a 'community of scholars', primarily dedicated to their own learning, to a place of learning where students are the primary, core, purpose of the university. But even more than this, for many universities, as we approach the twenty-first century, their role in the community is integral to their mission as an urban, a metropolitan, or a city university. This urban mission is not by any means confined to the former polytechnics, and nor does it come automatically from location in an urban context. Nevertheless, many of the former polytechnics do have a history which contributes to this mission. They draw on the traditions of the nineteenth-century technical, scientific, commercial, art and teacher education institutions which preceded them; on their strong links with industry, and their location in the physical centre of the town or city.

In the 1990s the impact of expansion in student numbers is seen in growing student cities -we could call them *UniverCities* – where a city of three- or four-hundred thousand people may have thirty thousand university students at its centre, and perhaps twice that with further education added. Swathes of the inner city may be given over to university buildings and student residences.

There always were universities in the middle of towns and cities. The difference now is that the urban university is conscious of its role as *a part of* – not *apart from* – the community. The urban university is closely woven into the fabric of the community; serving students, industry and business, and advancing knowledge and skills through teaching and research. The mixture of activities is not casual, nor without purpose and focus. On the contrary, it can tightly address a focused mission handed down from national educational objectives, in a role of active leadership and partnership. Already many universities take a lead in urban regeneration, bringing economic as well as educational and social benefits to the inner cities, in a broad mission of access, excellence and innovation. The role of the university as a resource and a generator helps to focus, not dilute, what it can achieve for individuals, society and the economy. Effective partnerships across public and private sectors will help the university and the community to thrive.

I hope you will not mind if I describe the role of the urban university from the perspective of the University of Sunderland, although the examples I use can, I am sure, be replicated in urban universities across the UK.

Sunderland, Britain's newest city, with a population of three hundred thousand people, has experienced the loss of traditional industries such as shipbuilding. It has experienced continuing unemployment of 12.5 per cent in the current recession, even given the spectacular successes of new industries and inward investment such as that of Nissan. Ninety-five per cent of companies on Wearside employ fewer than twenty people, and take-up of new technologies is patchy. Staying-on rates at school and college have increased in recent years but Sunderland, like the rest of the North East, has had, historically, the lowest participation in further and higher education. In the past, it was not necessary. You stepped out of school and crossed the road to the shipyards, or went down the pits. Now many agencies are working to shape a new Sunderland, creating employment and enterprise opportunities, and physically regenerating the city. All this gives the University a challenge, and a mission, in which the interests of the university and the interests of the community can coincide in a common purpose.

As a resource for the City the University's primary role is educational. The aim is to extend access to higher education, and to a higher education which is relevant to adult life and to employment. Our particular aim is to increase the base of students who come to us from Sunderland – currently 15 per cent, and 30 per cent from the North East – alongside our growth in national and international students. We form partnerships with our suppliers, in particular the colleges and the schools, to exert a 'pull factor' on mature people and school-leavers. Access courses, franchising arrangements, and a Sunderland Schools-University link project all contribute to the pull factor. The 'pull-through' to further and higher education is a key to extending awareness of the ladder of learning opportunities, and extending participation.

For the University, franchising is a way of decanting, increasing our physical capability in subjects of high demand, and stimulating demand in other areas. Franchising needs careful planning and support, but it is a friendly entry to higher education, a 'welcome mat' on the student's own doorstep.

Another way in which we can say 'come in: welcome to the university' is through progression arrangements, which will help us to identify students who can progress through the NVQ or GNVQ route to higher education. We also target the needs of particular groups. HITECC courses, and pre-access courses such as the *Hitch-hiker's Guide to Science and Technology* developed with the Open University, help those without a sufficient background in science and mathematics. An HND in Computing, specially designed for women returners, identifies personal needs as well as knowledge and skill needs, operating between the hours of 10.00 am and 3.00 pm. And, we have started to gain experience in targeting courses at students with special needs, such as the deaf.

Initial higher education is not the only story. The needs of individuals and industry for professional development and training, especially in technology, computing and management skills, have long been recognised in a range of standard or specially designed courses. In teacher training, and in professions allied to medicine, we help the practitioners and the professionals to further their knowledge and skills.

We also extend our sphere of influence beyond the city centre, in a dispersed urban and semi-rural area, by broadcasting learning beyond the university walls. *Wear FM* is the only campus-based community radio station in the UK. Located in one of our teaching buildings, it broadcasts twenty-four hours a day, seven days a week. *Wear FM* was funded initially by a range of agencies including the City Council, the Development Corporation, the TEC, and the business leadership team, Wearside Opportunity. The station is staffed by a small, professional team and an army of volunteers – volunteers called from the estates, literally by the voice of the radio, the new voice of Wearside. Students on the university's degree course in Communication Studies are able to operate the desks, and academic staff act as presenters for the university's slot. The station has developed an innovative scheduling of music, phone-ins, news and sport. We decided to enhance the training facility, so that the volunteers and students could be trained and accredited. *Wear FM* is a fully professional base for students, a training radio station – like a training hospital. We also use the station to pilot open learning: writing and broadcasting programmes for Bangladeshi women, and Kilcoyne's Chemistry, supported by learning packages.

Last year little *Wear FM* won the Sony Station of the Year Gold Award. What is important to us about *Wear FM* is that it is a partnership activity. It involves a broad section of the community and it straddles education, training, and leisure while helping to promote the confidence of the community and a pride in Sunderland. The radio station brings people into the university who, otherwise, would never have come. We use it for both outreach and inreach. It is an example of a multi-faceted urban regeneration project focused on regeneration through people, in the heart of the university and the heart of the city. *Wear FM* is a pilot in one medium, that of broadcast radio, for open and remote learning in the community. The university is now exploring teletext, cable and satellite, as well as remote computer links, which will take learning into the home and the workplace as well as colleges and schools, extending the university into the community.

The university also operates in the community through the application of its knowledge and expertise. The Industry Centre is the university's interface with industry and business, supporting innovation, and dedicated particularly to developing with other agencies an advanced manufacturing strategy for Wearside. The 'Make IT Grow' initiative aims to take one hundred companies and transform their IT capability by growing their own personnel, equipment and practice. The Business School's Quality Initiative retrains unemployed executives in quality management, who in turn can work with companies to put in place systems for BS5750. These initiatives, as well as nationally-led ones like the Teaching Company Scheme, do not merely transmit knowledge or apply technology – they transfer know-how through people, building back the resource into the region's industry. Research, development and innovation in a world of rapidly changing technology are key elements in

growth. Surveys show that the Northern region's share of significant innovation has fallen over time, reflecting a lack of research
and development facilities. The university, conscious of this
deficiency, is further extending its links with industry and seeking
support from UK and EC sources in order to exploit to the full its
wealth of scientific and technological expertise. In addition, in con-
junction with Wearside TEC, the commercial exploitation of new
ideas owned by graduates has been accommodated by an Innovation
Centre, where the technological and managerial aspects of trans-
lating new ideas into small company formation are successfully
undertaken.

The partnership with industry and business takes many forms. It
operates at the level of course design and delivery – a post-graduate
diploma for Pharmaceutical Quality Assurance has been developed
jointly with Glaxo, and a new degree in Automotive Design and
Manufacture has been launched with the support of Nissan and
other major employers. It involves the expertise of industrialists in
steering groups, on the board, as visiting professors. An extensive
network of partner relationships with industry, TECs, development
agencies, other educational institutions, and the community has
been established. More recently the 'Wearside in Europe' partnership has been formed with the TEC and the City Council to address
strategically the economic and social development of Wearside,
focusing especially on European funding opportunities.

Serving students, serving industry, serving the community – the
urban university has its part to play in enriching the life of the city
and its people. Social benefits include demographic rebalancing –
bringing young people back into the city and sustaining the life of
the city in the evenings – as well as geographical mobility – bringing
academic and other staff into the city. The university attracts students
and staff to the area and often retains them, counteracting a drift
to the south. A rapidly expanding university influences and
stimulates its environment in many ways, offering an increasingly
diverse range of educational, social and cultural opportunities,
extending the experience and raising the aspirations and self
confidence of the community.

We sponsored a Turner exhibition in Sunderland Museum, to the
benefit of local residents and school-children as well as our students.
Our students have formed an environmental project which is

creating nature spaces in particularly disadvantaged areas of the city. Together with Northumbria Police, our lecturers pioneered a Certificate in Stadium Crowd Management for Sunderland AFC. The Student Services department works with the city's Leisure Services department on joint sports projects .

The *economic* impact of the urban university is substantial and complex. Economic benefits derive from the organisation as an employer and as a consumer of services. Universities form a dynamic, major growth industry in the economy. They generate significant direct and indirect employment, income, export and investment effects which are transmitted through the whole economic system. Individually each university is a major economic enterprise within its own local economy, generating more employment and income than many industrial and commercial neighbours. The turnover of a university of, say, ten or twelve thousand students is the equivalent of a major business.

The economic impact can be calculated in terms of the direct and indirect jobs which a university generates, the new jobs brought by construction projects and by the suppliers who will expand to meet the needs of the total population of students and staff; and in terms of the money spent in the city on goods and services. With the recent expansion in higher education the economic impact of the urban university is highly visible. The biggest page one headline my university has had in the last year was **UNIVERSITY BRINGS 1,000 JOBS**. And why not?

The economic impact is real as well as visible – recent research by Durham University Business School suggests that the economic 'multiplier effect' of a university is greater than that of industry because of the structure of the turnover, and the proportion of expenditure by staff and students likely to come directly to the city.

The *physical* benefits of growth in higher education come in the development of new buildings, which in-fill and reclaim derelict industrial, residential or commercial areas, physically reshaping the environment. Investment in buildings and facilities provides a stimulus to the local economy and generates employment. The physical development, in our case of a new campus, is visible and real. It has a symbolic as well as an economic impact in regenerating the city. The location of our new campus, on the banks of the Wear, brings together history and hope for the future, on the site of the shipyards, beside St Peter's Church where it all began with Bede and Benedict Biscop. It is a campus designed to open out to the community in the heart of the city, transparent and permeable, expressing in its location, its architecture, and its portfolio of activities, the mission of a university of and for its city, shaping the new Sunderland.

Regeneration benefits the University. Whatever makes a city a better place in which to live and learn and work will attract students. And for us, for example, more than sixty per cent of our students come from outside the North, and ten per cent from outside the UK. Universities can rightly see themselves as more than an observer or a monitor on the sidelines of urban regeneration. They are a full player in the city team. The urban university takes a role of leadership in the community as well as service: shaping as well as monitoring, a facilitator of partnerships, an agent of change.

Are these two uncomfortably distinct or even contradictory missions – on the one hand access and the widening of participation in higher education, and on the other industrial application and innovation? Not at all, and certainly not in a city like Sunderland, where the project of growth and regeneration must focus on education and training as an investment for the future, as well as on employment and development. This diverse mission is essentially a focused and purposive mission for the advancement of knowledge through people. It assumes that technology transfer is a subset of knowledge transfer or learning transfer; that the advancement of knowledge lies through people – knowledgeable, capable people; that there is a cumulative, incremental learning gain, at the level of the individual, the company and the community; and that the university itself gains. The interface with industry and business brings us new knowledge and expertise which is then built into the learning base, so that we can add it back in, to the benefit of the community. This is the *learning spin-off*, the learning *multiplier effect*.

Is this mission parochial, inward looking, unrelievedly local? No. It uses location and context as a strength and deploys this actively as integral to the university's overall strategy, operating from a firm, rooted base. In Sunderland, it certainly does not mean taking only local students or undertaking research only for local businesses; but Sunderland is where we start from, and all our national and international activity will come back to and strengthen that base, helping to sustain development in the North East.

This is essentially a coherent and purposive approach to a broad role in the community. And this purposive approach can equally be applied at regional, or national level, as well as within the city. The principles of focus, of identifying stakeholders and players, of partnership, of giving and gaining, and of a common purpose remain the same. They have meaning equally for the role of a university in its city, and a higher education system in its national community.

Universities of the Future

I would like to conclude this end-of-the-twentieth-century view of universities in the community by posing a few questions for the future.

Let me start with students. Who will they be? Universities of the twenty-first century will, I hope, be peopled by students who regard themselves as learning throughout their lives, and who expect, confidently, to use the resource of the university many times, updating their knowledge and skills. They will come from a wider base and from more diverse routes. They will expect a range of support services, from child-care to recreational facilities. Quality of learning, as perceived by the learners, together with the standards expected by awarding bodies and employers, will be the key to success. Students will certainly expect high value from their higher education – a quality service to meet their learning needs.

What will those learning needs be? How can universities better meet the needs of students and employers in the next century? Can we envisage a new structure of academic and vocational higher education? There will, perhaps, be a clearer understanding and a clearer definition of occupationally relevant subjects and programmes. We may yet have an umbrella of qualifications which bridges the academic/vocational divide, gives parity of esteem to vocational achievement, and develops work and life competences in academic programmes. Bernard Shaw said that 'people don't have their virtues and vices in sets, they have them anyhow, all mixed'. Perhaps we could, in similar vein, recognise that individuals may benefit from concurrent academic and vocational higher education – the one giving immediate occupational competence, the other a long-term flexibility and growth potential. We could extend, say, the mix of Engineering and Language in the same degree programme to something rather like an HNC in Engineering alongside a half BA Hons in Philosophy.

What changes are likely in the way courses are designed and delivered? I am sure we will see more two-year programmes, whether accelerated or intensive degree programmes or diplomas, not only because of advantages to institutions in increased efficiency, but because these will meet the needs of the diverse student population. As in other areas of consumer demand, high added value attaches to speed, a fast service. And, continuing the analogy with consumer goods, where quality is a function of speed plus cus-tomisation or personalisation, I am sure we will see personal learning portfolios, created and negotiated through credits and the modular programmes which will be in place in most, if not all, universities.

Turning to delivery, universities will need, above all, to be responsive, developing a flexible and elastic delivery which per-sonalises the learning programme, overcoming time and space constraints. This means not merely the adjustment of the academic year – that is more in the interests of the supplier than the users – but the introduction of strategies which genuinely allow indepen-dent, active learning while preserving the core of the precious relationship between learner and tutor.

What are the implications of innovation in teaching and learning and of new technologies for 'universities without walls'? An expanded higher education system calls for a creative review of the learning infrastructure in order to deliver quality of learning. The concept and usage of library, computing and learning resources may undergo a transformation, with learning support for all students provided creatively and *variably* – not only in terms of the media which are used, but in their distribution and delivery. Already we have consortia, regional and national, providing course materials. Access to international information systems from the academic's or the student's workstation is already possible. The concept of the 'virtual library' – the electronic library – is being actively developed. This goes a step beyond the national and international networking of information which we have so far seen. The 'virtual classroom' is already with us via satellite and other media for remote learning. The electronic campus is already virtually a reality.

The 'Virtual University', totally personalised in the home or the workplace, real-time and fully interactive, may become a global reality for learning, for research, and high level global academic dialogue and conferencing. Virtual, of course, not in the sense of approximation to reality, but in the virtue – the strength – of its educational, academic and research capability.

The university community of the twenty-first century university may indeed be global as well as local – bringing us back to the definition of the university as an international 'community of scholars'. Would that move us completely away from the model of the urban university, closely interwoven in the fabric of the community? Perhaps so: probably not. But I will pause here for a little digression about Padua. A couple of years ago, I visited the University of Padua with a small British Council delegation, and I was struck by two quite separate experiences. One was Galileo's anatomy theatre, perfectly encased, free-standing inside the structure – a university within a university, history within history. The other, however, was even more singular. We crossed from the University, just a few steps, to the City Hall, where the Mayor proudly told us of the agreement he had just signed with the Rector. The University and the City – an agreement, a common purpose, and after just three hundred years or so! The idea – the role – of a university does change and develop, and ideas have their moment.

Well, disregard the alluring technologies of the virtual university. With or without technology, the university is expanding beyond its walls, and its role in the community will shift and change. Will universities in the twenty-first century be the sole provider of higher education? Franchising already spreads the provider role, and we may wish to think further about the articulation and the definition of further and higher education. School-based teacher training could be extended to other professions – as, of course, advanced apprenticeships have operated in the past. Companies, either on their own, or working in close partnerships with the universities, may themselves take on the role of provider. After all, they do so at the moment to some extent in training, in supervising post-graduate research, in sandwich placements and in industry-based projects. As workplace learning increases, industry itself may provide the learners and be the provider as well as the employer.

The university may, then, become less of an institution, more a focal point, an agency, a facilitator, with learning taking place partly or mainly elsewhere. The core resource, and the generator, will still be the university; and the university's core resource will remain its academics and their expertise. But there may be a shift, away from the institution, to a dispersed community of life-long learners. If this does happen in the twenty-first century the wheel will have turned full circle – from a community of scholars, with their hoard of knowledge inside the monastery walls, to a living 'learning community' – the university extended, permeating the community. Well, that would not be too bad a vision for the millennium, would it?

Discussion

Professor Peter Mortimore (Institute of Education, University of London): You have painted a very glowing picture but I wonder if you could tell us a little of the other side. There must be some awkwardnesses, tensions and dilemmas which have to be resolved. Perhaps you could tell us about links with the longer-established universities in your region and with your community, especially its unemployed members.

Dr Wright: The North East is characterised by a great cohesiveness and a very strong sense of collaboration and competition, not only in education. Before the binary divide was abolished the higher education institutions in the region enjoyed good relationships with each other, and we established a framework organisation to work together, particularly in providing support for industry through research. We recognised that there was a strong element of competition as well and, in a sense, the bringing together of former polytechnics and the universities in a new sector intensifies that competition. But there is no doubt that we recognise that we need to work together to make higher education provision for the region. There are undoubtedly tensions but the important thing is to try – as in negotiating skills – to identify the common ground. It is also important that we try to focus on a particular mission. The mission that I have described is not necessarily that of the other universities in the region. They are all slightly different and it may well be that we shall each focus more precisely as we go forward.

As far as the community is concerned, there are tensions – in Sunderland, as in many university cities. It is quite possible for a university or college to be in the middle of its city and not 'be' there. An institution which takes the view that it just happens to be in a particular location, but does not necessarily connect with it, will have a different mission -international, for example. But, if you want to make those connections and to be a university in the community it is important both to recognise the tensions and to recognise the various interests of all the players, and where those interests coincide. Higher education and training is a choice made by society and for society and we need to find our place in the light of that choice. I would regard it as a responsibility to find a common interest with the community, whether it is the city or industry and business as a whole.

Unemployment is an enormous challenge for the whole community in Wearside, but there are ways of approaching it. The university has a responsibility as well as an opportunity in that. The area is one where unemployment goes back a long time, and where participation in further and higher education has traditionally been low. It might seem anomalous to find a university which seems at least to be extremely affluent – of course we are not in fact – in the middle of an area where there is a great deal of unemployment. That view is expressed. We have to work through and with that, partly recognising that we are trying to make a better base of education and training for future generations, and partly by jumping generations – providing for unemployed people to come into further and higher education – mature people, the parents and even the grandparents of the young people who are coming forward. There is nothing like direct experience of higher education to give people an awareness of what it really can do for them.

Our new campus is on the shipyards, which is very painful. By St Peter's church it is very pleasant, but across the road is a school which is fairly disadvantaged. I do not expect that many children from that school currently think they will ever go to a university. Our campus will be completed in 2003. By then, it should be as natural and expected for children to step across the road into our campus as it was to step into shipyards or go down the pits. That gives us a role and a mission, but between now and 2003 it may not be easy.

Lord Walton: I remember my boyhood in the North East, where in many ways excellent families would look mystified when someone suggested that their sons or daughters might even consider going on to higher education. Why were they not going out to get a job? That was the attitude that existed at that time. To some extent it has carried over into an anti-education ethos in some communities. 'Higher education is not for the likes of us.' I am glad to hear that Dr Wright is trying to tackle that situation in her community. It is still pervasive but to a lesser extent than in the past.

Angela Crum-Ewing (University of Reading): I found your address most inspiring. One of the things that was so refreshing for me was that you did not once mention how all this is going to be afforded. I would be very interested to know your views are on how society is going to manage to accomplish this future which I am sure we all want. How is this higher education system which is going to be open to the community to be afforded?

Dr Wright: You quite rightly call me to question. It does seem to me that the one-in-three goal for higher education is a choice made by society – and made very wisely – recognising that we need to invest in the future through people. The question is how that choice is going to be translated into investment and who is going to make it.We have set ourselves a very big task. If we go on with the present situation where, very desirably, many students travel away from home, for example, the role that gives to the universities is potentially to sustain all the learning and life expectations of 30% of that age cohort. One of my fears is that their natural expectations for a range of learning support, welfare and recreational services will put too great a pressure on the universities. I spoke about stakeholders, and it seems to me that one of the ways forward is to look at how we can call on the various stakeholders to contribute to the overall higher education system. We do have to look at a new funding base and recognise the part played by the various stakeholders. I think we have to face up to that.

There are ways in which that can be addressed. A university – or more than one university – in a large city will bring together a very large proportion of an age cohort and many local students in an area which already has many amenities and facilities provided by the city. We need to consider how far those facilities and amenities should be separate and how far they can overlap. The demands we face at the moment are demands on one public sector department, because we are mainly funded from the DFE. But also there are needs which are being provided through other routes, through the local authorities. We have to look at the distribution of effort and of responsibility.

Higher education has got to be affordable, but the proportion of GDP that is currently devoted to it will not sustain it into the twenty-first century. Some way has got to be found, and unless there is going to be a greater proportion of GDP there will have to be another stakeholder identified, whether it is individuals or some other source.

Robin Tulloch (Academic Secretary, Oxford Brookes University): Bede and Benedict Biscop would have had no doubts about their mission. They were keeping alive a small flame in what seemed a dark world: a flame of culture. I think we are in danger, as universities, of continuing to follow that mission without changing very much. When we come to 30% or perhaps half of the population going through higher education we will have to take account of the needs of those from ethnic and socio-economic groups not normally represented in universities. We are not yet very good at defining what their needs are, and one of the reasons is that it is very difficult to grasp 'the community'. To some extent it is an artificial construct. I am very concerned to get these groups into our universities, but I am not sure that we yet know enough about what we will be teaching them.

Dr Wright: The expansion of higher education and the more diverse entrants which that will bring coincides with a move towards a demand for quality by consumers. This is a happy coincidence. If the pressure for change does not come from inside the universities, it will come from people voicing what they would like and want. Certain universities will have to be more responsive. We are often asked what one in three will mean in higher education, and whether it will lower standards. The answer to that is that it will not because we will maintain the standards. All it means is exactly what it says: that one in three people will go into higher education. But it will mean that we must, as you say, make sure that we are providing for the needs and interests of all the very diverse people who will by definition be entering into our universities. We have to listen very hard to those people who are coming in and to recognise that not only will they have needs which are not currently delivered by the universities but that those needs may represent more genuinely the needs of individuals and our society than we expect. One of the keys to this is to think of universities as teaching people rather than teaching subjects, because if you think in terms of people it changes the spectrum. You stop thinking: 'this is the subject which is going to be handed on'. Instead you say: 'these are the people who want to learn.'

It is difficult to grasp a broad concept like 'the community'. 'The community' is a phrase which comes and goes in its popularity and acceptability. It has different meanings at different times. But if you translate it into various groups and into various initiatives, then it starts to become real and concrete. I referred earlier to Wear FM. Another thing we have looked at is cable TV. Our research showed us was that there was again a coincidence, though it looked at first like a contradiction. In asking who watches cable TV and what kind of audiences it has, on the face of it, it seemed like they are not the sort of audiences to want education. But turn that round and that becomes precisely the opportunity. If what we are trying to do is raise the participation of local people in further and higher education – and that means extending to socio-economic groups who are not currently represented – those are precisely the groups who actually watch cable TV. So it gives us a way into what may seem a very amorphous thing, the community. We can actually get there with something which goes directly into people's homes and does meet their needs because what they want to do is to watch TV.

Martin Tims (Esso UK, plc): Most of what you have been saying has been looking at the supply side of universities rather than the demand side. I would question whether the 30% level is applicable willy-nilly. What worries me is the difficulty of ensuring that the output of universities is matched to the demands of employers. What I think we are currently seeing is a radical re-think among young people because so many recent graduates cannot get jobs. I hope it is a short term effect of the recession but some graduate recruiters are saying there has been a radical restructuring of employment in industry and that there are not, therefore, the same opportunities for the traditional graduates as in the past. To some extent it is a joint problem. Industry must do more, but equally universities must do more to ensure more science and engineering graduates. My worry is that we are in grave danger, at the moment, of building an underclass of very disillusioned graduates, very articulate, but with a massive chip on their shoulder.

Dr Wright: Obviously it is a worry that many graduates are now unemployed. Part of that worry has actually been with us for quite some time. It is a real effect now, and it is on a larger scale than previously. But it has always been the case that many graduates do not enter into permanent employment for some considerable time and I am sure we shall accustom people to view higher education as lasting a lifetime – not a once and for all experience – from now on. The benefits last a lifetime, so one must take a longer view.

The goal that has been set – very carefully – is for one in three young people to enter higher education. It is up to the universities, with industry bodies, to look at the range of programmes and awards offered. We should not assume that one in three entering higher education means one in three doing the kinds of degree we currently offer. We have to look at a different range of qualifications for all kinds of reasons – partly, as you say, to make sure that people who leave higher education for the first time are ready for employment. I believe in that firmly. At the same time – and I hear employers saying this – we must make sure that people also have the potential for growth and the flexibility to enable them to progress to new situations.

Lord Walton: All the discussions we have had at the National Commission on Education with organisations like the CBI and similar bodies have indicated the crucial importance of broadening the range of qualifications in a society which is going to be increasingly skills-based in the future. Dr Wright is surely correct in saying that universities have to examine that carefully.

Sir Randolph Quirk (Wolfson Foundation): There are all kinds of reasons why there should be graduate unemployment at the moment. Partly it is that universities have been turning out graduates of the kind that there are no jobs for. Who wants a historian or a sociologist in ICI? Secondly, even with relatively career-oriented degrees like engineering we have had too few engineering firms that have been ambitious enough to employ graduate engineers. What you have been saying coincides with a really major change: namely, the whole concept of the university as a degree-awarding machine is going to have to change. There is nothing 'pie in the sky' about expecting a participation rate of 30% or 40%. We have it already in the United States and Japan. What matters is that people go to university, not because it is a way of staying off the dole, but because there are short courses in this that or the other, something that is going to be useful or indeed something that is merely interesting at the time.

What you were saying about the role of the university in the community and life-long education is very important. We still think in terms of the 18-21 year old who leaves Newcastle to go to Bristol or leaves Bristol to go to Hull and never returns there, making an absolute break in the community between those who have university education and those who have not. What we are now talking about is a community where every member of a family will have had some contact with higher education and where it will become increasingly known that it is absolutely essential for social, career and professional development to have it.

Dr Wright: Modular programmes will help – simply by making it possible to go in and out easily. We have to look at the shape of programmes. One of the difficulties the universities encounter in engineering is recruiting people, whether to a B.Eng. or an HND programme. Engineering does not have the status of other professions in society. Also, again because of status, people aspire to whatever is the highest award they can get accepted for. This is a mistake and some way has to be found of getting away from the very artificial values which can be attached to particular kinds of award. What students want from full time higher education is to do something which is going to interest and intrigue them and which they like, whether it is history, philosophy or anything else. Most students do want to get a job, but at the moment they are faced with very much an either/or. Of course we do also have to talk to employers and make sure we are providing for the needs of the manufacturing base and service sector and so on.

Encouragingly, I have noticed in talking to schools in Sunderland – schools where the staying- on rate past 16 is currently abysmally low – that, if you tell them about NVQs and GNVQs, both parents and children are interested, and so are the schools. We have to go out and make sure we are genuinely able to meet that demand in a way that attracts people. One of the things that happens when you create modular programmes and credit transfer arrangements and start describing to people the way they can come in and out, and do things in little chunks, is that the first group of people that understands that is not actually the 18-year-olds coming in but the people who work in the university. They really do understand about it. I do not think there is a difficulty once we get over the barrier of creating a demand.

Lord Walton: If you study the qualifications and backgrounds of the leaders of major companies in the UK you will find a very high concentration of accountants. There is nothing wrong with having accountants at the head of these organisations but if you look at similar organisations in Japan, Germany and France you will find many more scientists, engineers and others who have that kind of background. It is a curious facet of our society that this has happened over the years.

Jane Harrop (NCVQ): I welcome your comments about the linkage between education and training and the future role of graduates. From my experience as a former university administrator in the University of Virginia I recognise many good features of the American system in your description. But there are aspects of the US system which I hope we will avoid. One is the isolation which happens to undergraduates within that academic community. They become isolated from the community in general. It seems to me that you are making an effort to avoid that. A division sometimes also arises in the US system between undergraduate and graduate education. Postgraduate students became increasingly divorced from the rest. Yet these are the future lecturers and professors and the separation, perhaps, tends to reinforce the stereotypes.

Dr Wright: If there is that separation between undergraduate and postgraduate and if there is isolation, it is the university's job to do something about it, both by getting a sense of community and identity for postgraduates and by getting a sense of articulation between undergraduate and postgraduate. Postgraduate education is one of the features of the expanding system that we have to address. We have to think about the generations to come and the people who are going to provide the learning – that is the academics – and make sure that they are appropriately equipped for that future. I agree with you entirely that they, too, must not be isolated.

In my university at the moment it would be very hard for under-graduates to be isolated from the community. They just spill all over the place, particularly this year. We have forty-eight buildings, spread over about two square miles of city centre. In some ways it is a tremendous problem if you view it as a fragmented university with isolated pockets of people in various places. But if you see all these students milling around the place and see it as permeating the community, it takes on quite a different perspective. It is that which leads me to start to think about the relationship between students and other people in the community – young or old – and the way in which we share amenities. I think that a separation within the community is the worst of all worlds. If we are going to be there, we really have to be in, and with, the community.

6
Scholarship Reconsidered: Priorities for a New Century

Dr Ernest Boyer: President, The Carnegie Foundation for the Advancement of Teaching, Princeton, New Jersey.

I am greatly honoured to participate in this distinguished lecture series which considers prospects for the university in the century ahead. Universities all around the world have been profoundly influenced by those elegant institutions of higher learning that took root here in the United Kingdom nearly a millennium ago. Standards of excellence were established at Oxford and at Cambridge that have contributed enduringly to humanity's social, civic and intellectual progress, and academic leaders in every nation are profoundly in your debt for establishing, here in England, the tradition of distinguished scholarship that remains a model for us all.

The Changing Role of Higher Education

I should like to consider the future of the university from the perspective of my own country, and to attempt to predict the future. But before doing so, I should like to reflect a little on the past and recall how the role of higher learning in America has changed throughout the years. When little Harvard College was founded in 1636, inspired as you know by Emmanuel College, Cambridge, the focus was on the student. Teaching was a central, even a sacred function, and the highest accolade that a professor could receive was the one which Chaucer extended to the Oxford Cleric, when he said:

And gladly would he learn, and gladly teach.

110

Educating the whole person was at the very heart of the Colonial College and, for a century and a half, that was what scholarship in America was all about. Even as late as 1869, when Charles Eliot assumed the Presidency of Harvard, he declared in his inaugural address that the primary business of the American professor must be 'regular and assiduous classroom teaching'.

A change was in the wind and, early in the nineteenth century, the focus of American higher education slowly began to shift from the shaping of young lives to the building of a nation. In 1824, Rensselaer Polytechnic Institute (RPI) was founded in Troy, New York, and, according to historian Fred Rudolph, RPI was a constant reminder that America needed rail-road builders, bridge builders, and builders of all kinds. The now famous Land Grant Act of 1862 linked higher learning to America's agricultural and technical revolution, and when social critic Lincoln Stephens visited Madison in 1909 he declared that 'in Wisconsin the university is as close to the intelligent farmer as his pig-pen or his tool-house'. At the turn of the century, David Starr Jordan, the newly appointed president of Stanford University declared that 'the entire university movement in this country is toward reality and practicality'. And on the East Coast Charles Eliot, who was still at Harvard after forty years, said that 'serviceability' is the central mission of American higher education. Frankly, I find it quite amazing that just one hundred years ago the words 'reality', 'practicality', and 'serviceability' were used by America's most distinguished academic leaders to describe the mission of higher education. To put it simply the scholarship of teaching had been joined by the scholarship of building.

Meanwhile a third tradition was beginning to emerge. The Lawrence Scientific School at Harvard, and the Sheffield Scientific School at Yale began to direct the work of scholarship from the classroom and the farm field to the laboratory, and in 1861 Yale University granted the first PhD degree ever awarded in the United States. During the same period American academics who studied at the great German universities of Göttingen, Heidelberg and Humboldt were profoundly influenced by the emerging scholarship of science. In 1876 Daniel Coit Gilman founded Johns Hopkins University in Maryland and sought to replicate the German model. When Princeton University President, Woodrow Wilson, spoke at Gilman's retirement two decades later he described Johns Hopkins as the first university in America where the discovery of truth was judged superior to mere teaching. And I suspect that was the first moment where the teaching versus research debate actually began.

Thus, in two hundred and fifty years, higher learning in America had gone from the Colonial College tradition with its emphasis on the student, on general knowledge, and on loyalty to the campus, to the German university tradition with its emphasis not on the student but on the professoriate; not on general knowledge but specialised knowledge; not on loyalty to the campus but loyalty to the guild. Still, with all its appeal, the Johns Hopkins model remained the exception not the rule and, well in to the twentieth century, America continued to take great pride in the diversity of institutions that ranged from liberal arts colleges, to land grant colleges, to the emerging centres of research.

Following World War II, however, we experienced a veritable sea-change in higher education in the United States. With the passage of the GI Bill America moved, in Martin Trow's vivid formulation, from élite to mass higher education. Almost over-night, access and equality of opportunity became the new public policies for the nation. And while the GIs who returned from the war considered going on to college a great privilege, their children, and surely their grandchildren, embraced it as a right. Today, access to higher education is assumed to be an obligation that everyone has the right eagerly to pursue. And currently, about sixty per cent of all secondary school leavers are going on to some form of higher education. This is more than double the percentage that existed before the second world war.

The irony is that, at the very time that the social policy in our country was becoming more egalitarian and being broadened, and as we were opening college doors, the rewards system for the professoriate, and the symbols of institutional success, were being narrowed. Access and diversity were still being praised but, below the surface, American higher education was rapidly becoming not an expansive but a more narrowly-defined, imitative system. Service in the Land Grant tradition was no longer honoured. Teaching in the Colonial College tradition was no longer well rewarded. Research and publication, these were emerging as the dominant measures of success, for both institutions and for professors. Now, the community colleges and selected liberal arts institutions continued to take great pride in the distinctiveness of their mission, but a host of other institutions in our country, especially those which we classify as 'doctorate-granting' and 'comprehensives' – which are primarily those which are offering masters but not doctorate degrees – began to measure themselves not by their own distinctive purpose, nor by the more egalitarian trends that were becoming the social policy of the nation. They began to measure themselves by the Johns Hopkins and the Berkeley research model, creating an American higher education which sociologist David Riesman called 'a snakelike procession'. In 1968, Talcott Parsons captured the spirit of this period when he wrote 'today the typical professor now resembles the scientist more than the gentleman-scholar of an earlier generation'.

I might add, parenthetically, that in the 1960s I was at the University of California, Santa Barbara, and I watched a former teacher training and home economics institution being folded into the prestigious University of California system. It was a wrenching process to watch as faculty expectations were being dramatically redefined. Faculty, who had been hired to perform teaching and service missions, were suddenly being held accountable to a standard in which publication mattered most. I then joined the State University of New York where we struggled to protect the diversity of a sixty-four campus system at the very time colleges were determined to move up the prestige ladder by imitating the research institution just above them.

Growing Dissatisfaction

Out of this great diversity of our background, therefore, at least three major strands of influence were created – the teaching, the service, and the research model. At the very time when we expanded our commitment, rather than having institutions being judged against diverse measures, they were being judged against a unitary model. But as it turned out, large numbers of both faculty and students became dissatisfied with the narrowness of this definition. Students, especially the undergraduates in our country, felt frustrated by a system where teaching was undervalued. They resented being taught by graduate students, not professors. They complained about large lectures halls where teaching could be monitored only by the television screen overhead. And it is revealing that, according to recent Carnegie Foundation surveys, about half the undergraduates in our country say they feel like a number in a book, and sixty percent say their professors have no interest in their personal lives or who they are. Such dissatisfaction, of course, runs dramatically counter to the tradition of the Colonial College which we like to keep alive, at least in the 'view books' when we are out recruiting students.

The view books still convey this image of a familial community in which students are guaranteed that, if they enrol, they will get tender, loving care. When we did the book *College* I surveyed thirty view books, and I was impressed with the repetitiveness with which the words 'family' and 'community' found their way into the language. Indeed, I then studied all the pictures, and I was impressed that they, too, conveyed this close connection between faculty and students. From the pictures alone, I concluded that about sixty per cent of all classes in America are held outside, underneath a tree, by a gently flowing stream. The only problem is that some of these students actually enrol and they can find that the Colonial College culture has been replaced by yet another model. The freshmen and sophomores, in particular, feel that they are lonely individuals in the wilderness, and only when they declare a major and enrol in graduate studies do they feel that the faculty and student cultures begin to come together.

In order to sustain the Colonial College traditions in America, what we have created is a support staff made up of deans of students, residence hall advisors, counsellors and health clinics. They all keep the student culture well served, while the professoriate is committed increasingly to the academic life. This has divided our campuses between learning in the classroom and low grade decadence outside.

Dissatisfaction can be found, incidentally, among the professoriate as well. According to Carnegie Foundation surveys which we have conducted since 1968, about sixty per cent of the faculty in our country say they would rather teach than do research. In comparison, a survey of faculty here in England reveals that about forty per cent of the faculty prefer teaching to research. Two-thirds of all faculty in the US say that teaching effectiveness, not publication, should be the primary basis for promotion, and in the 1990 survey nearly seventy per cent of all the professors in our country said that we need better ways, beside publication, to measure faculty performance. What has emerged is an interesting definition of the role of the professoriate and, while the success of the faculty has been judged increasingly by research and publication, our surveys suggest that great restiveness lies just below the surface.

Especially disturbing is the critical attitude toward higher education that is developing beyond the campus. If this were only an internal quarrel I think it would not be so troublesome. But there is an uncertainty about the role of higher education in society at large. In recent years, we have had a steady stream of critical publications in the US – from *The Closing of the American Mind* to *Profscam* – books that have convinced large sections of our society that faculty are self-serving and unresponsive, and that college students are paying more and getting less. Increasingly, policy-makers and politicians view higher education as a private benefit not a public good. They see the campus as a place where faculty get tenured, and students get credentialed, but they see little relationship between the overall work of the university, and the nation's pressing social, civic and economic problems.

Further, the severe recession in our country has placed higher education in sharp competition with the schools, with health care institutions, and with welfare programmes. This has led to some of the most dramatic budget cutbacks in recent years. In some states faculty are being discharged, required courses cancelled. Student fees are sky-rocketing. And most ominous perhaps, enrolments are being cut at the very moment when more afro-american and hispanic students are clamouring to get in. We are planting the seeds of huge social unrest, because repeatedly we hear from our minority constituencies 'you are changing the ground rules at the very time when our children wish to take advantage of the opportunities you provide'. Indeed, about thirty percent of all of the students of the nation's public schools are now from a minority group. In California and the south west it is fifty percent or more. The face of America is changing at the very time when there is a capping of the options, and when the commitment to open enrolment seems to be diminished. Just last week I was in California, and every respected academic leader with whom I spoke, including Clark Kerr, expressed grave doubt that California's famous Master Plan, which served as a model for the nation, will, in the next decade, continue to be supported.

To put this diagnosis into perspective, let me say that, overall, America's system of higher education is alive and well, especially when compared to other institutions. And yet, for the first time in half a century, the social contract between university and society is being sharply challenged, and the two central features of our system – access and diversity – are, at this moment in our history, danger-ously at risk.

Renewing the Universities

This brings me to the future. Given current tensions, is it possible to bring a new sense of vitality and purpose to higher learning? Is it possible to strengthen public confidence, and to create, for the twenty-first century, institutions of consequence and social influence? If so, how is this to be accomplished?

In a recent Carnegie Foundation Report, entitled *Scholarship Reconsidered* we conclude that the university will be renewed only as we give new meaning and new insight to scholarship itself. It cannot be externally imposed. It has to grow out of the work of the professoriate, by defining adequately and sufficiently the role of academic life. The time has come to move beyond the tired old teaching-versus-research debate, and begin to explore the more essential issue: what does it mean to be a scholar? In response to that compelling question we propose a four part paradigm of schol-arship, one that defines an appropriate agenda, not only for the professor, but for the university in the twenty-first century.

The Scholarship of Discovery

What will be the characteristics of scholarship in the coming century? First, we say in our report that research is at the very heart of academic life, and we celebrate what we call *the scholarship of discovery*. Research will always be central to the work of higher learning, and in the century ahead, universities must continue to support and provide a home for this essential function. Indeed, I am increasingly troubled by the growth of corporate sponsored research in the US. We now have contractual arrangements in which corporations have prior claim on all the discoveries that can be profitably directed toward their industry. If this is allowed to spread, it seems to me, it will seriously compromise the integrity of scholarly investigation. I believe absolutely that the weight of scholarly research should stay within the academy itself. Fifty years ago, Vannevar Bush, who was the President of MIT and the first Director of the National Science Foundation, put it this way. He said:

> Universities are the well-spring of human knowledge and understanding, and as long as they are vigorous and healthy, and as long as they support scientists who are free to pursue truth wherever it may lead, there will continue to be a flow of new scientific knowledge.

To put it simply, while industry conducts research, and while collaboration is essential, it is my own judgement that universities and research belong together.

The dilemma is, however, that not every college can define research as its central mission, which has been the inclination in the US in the past twenty to thirty years. I have talked to at least sixty university presidents who are sure that by the end of the century they will be in the top twenty. It is going to be a very crowded field! We have about 3,000 plus universities and colleges in America, and I think we are going to have to make some very hard decisions. Federal research support has flattened out. At the present time, only about ten per cent of all the proposals that pass peer review can be funded from the federal grants that are available. And so, it is quite clear that some hard choices must be made. While a few high-quality research projects may be funded on many campuses, it seems obvious that the number of research-intensive institutions in our country must be dramatically restricted. The American Association of Universities, which defines itself as the academic *crème de la crème* is comprised of only sixty institutions. But somewhere between sixty and one hundred and twenty will become the institutions – the research-intensive centres – in which research is in fact the central mission. The goal is not to diminish the significance of research, but to protect it, and to ensure that free enquiry of the highest quality remains a centre-piece of the university in the century ahead.

The Scholarship of Integration

In addition to the scholarship of discovery, the Carnegie Report also proposes what is called *the scholarship of integration*. In the coming century, there will be an urgent need for scholars who go beyond the isolated facts; who make connections across the disciplines; and who begin to discover a more coherent view of knowledge and a more integrated, more authentic, view of life. Barbara McClintock, the Nobel laureate, said on one occasion that 'everything is one'. 'There is' she said ' no way to draw a line between things'. And yet the disciplinary fragmentation that now dominates the academic culture runs almost completely counter to this sense of wholeness. Frank Press, the President of the National Academy of Sciences, suggested recently that the scientist is in some respects an artist. He illustrated this by pointing out that the magnificent double helix, which broke the genetic code is not only rational, it is beautiful as well. Perhaps, then, scientists and artists are looking for relationships and patterns. Maybe, beyond the intellectual quest there is an aesthetic satisfaction. Yet, on most campuses, the arts and the sciences function in wholly separate worlds. Several years ago when the world renowned physicist, Victor Weisskopf, was asked 'what gives you hope in troubled times?' he replied: ' Mozart and quantum mechanics'. But, where in our fragmented academic culture can scholars begin to make connections such as these?

I am convinced that there is a silver lining and that in the twenty-first century, at the very time that we talk about specialisation, we will begin to see patterns of great convergence. More than at any other time in recent memory, researchers feel the need to move beyond traditional disciplinary boundaries. Indeed, some of the most exciting work in the academy today is in what might be called the 'hyphenated disciplines' – in psycho-linguistics, in bio-engineering, and the like. New disciplines are being formed simply because old boxes do not fit the new intellectual questions, and because the social imperatives outside call for inter-disciplinary connections. Connections are being made in what Michael Polanyi calls 'the over-lapping academic neighbourhoods'. Anthropologist Clifford Goetz goes so far as to describe the shifts within the fields of knowledge as 'fundamental reconfigurations'. He says that something is happening to the way we think about the way we think.

Looking to the next century we will need universities that give priority to the scholarship of integration – institutions with cross-disciplinary institutes, with all-college forums and with a vibrant programme of general education for their students. Such universities will also be places where philosophers, scientists and artists join together to discover common ground, and seek to put their learning in historical, social and ethical perspective. To put it quite simply, I think the challenge of the next century is not only the discovery of knowledge, but fitting those discoveries into a larger pattern and perspective so that we can move from information to knowledge, and from knowledge, perhaps, to wisdom. Over fifty years ago Mark Van Doren wrote that 'the connectedness of things' is what the educator contemplates to the limit of his capacity. Van Doren concludes by saying that the student who can begin early in life to see things as connected, has begun the life of learning. And this, it seems to me, is what scholarship in the twenty-first century will be about.

The Scholarship of Application

Beyond the scholarship of discovery and of integration, however, universities in the next century also must be committed to the *scholarship of application*. The first two dimensions of scholarship reflect the investigative and synthesising functions of academic life. The third element, application, moves toward engagement, and defines the campus not as an isolated island, but as a staging-ground for action. Professor Donald Short at MIT writes about what he calls 'the reflective practitioner', and he argues that scholars not only move from theory to practice, but also from practice back to theory.

There is an increasing trend in education, in professional schools in particular, towards building the theory of their field in the practice that students experience at the very outset. Harvard's new medical school programme, called New Pathways, puts new students not into the classroom, but into the clinic, and then they go back from the clinic to formulate the theories of good practice. Business schools increasingly engage students in the real field of work. Law practice follows the same model. And anyone engaged in the preparation of the teacher knows how dramatically the theories of the classroom are redefined once you move into a third grade classroom and encounter students. The reciprocity then is from theory to practice, and from practice back to theory. This is redefined, sharpened and honed, and the more it is based upon experience in the field, the more adequate it becomes.

If we view practice, or service, from this perspective, it means that service – the application of knowledge – will not only improve society, it will improve the quality of scholarship itself. In the coming century, the university must be more attentive to the scholarship of application. We need, in the US at least, a national network of what I might call service universities -institutions that relate scholarship to the needs of schools, industry, health clinics, and the inner cities – just as the Land Grant colleges served agriculture and industry a century ago.

About fifteen years ago, about a dozen or more of our large city-based universities formed what were called the 'Urban Grant' universities, trying to model their vision after the Land Grant universities. The hope was to take the intellectual life of the community and engage it in the churning pathologies of our inner cities. And I think, if such connections are not authentically established, that the prospects for both the universities and society at large will be dramatically diminished. The university cannot be disengaged from the challenges of the century ahead. Harvard historian Oscar Hammer put the challenge this way: 'Our troubled planet can no longer afford the luxury of pursuits confined to the ivory tower. Scholarship has to prove its worth: not on its own terms, but by service to the nation and the world'.

The Scholarship of Teaching

Scholarship at its best not only means discovering, integrating and applying knowledge. It also means transmitting knowledge – a process we call the *scholarship of teaching*. The simple truth is that the work of the professoriate becomes of consequence only insofar as it is understood by others. Since teaching is, as Aristotle put it, 'the highest form of understanding', it is through the influence of great teachers that the flame of scholarship is kept alive from one generation to the next. I suspect that almost all of us are here today because of the inspiration of a master teacher. I remember three or four who genuinely changed my life. The fascinating point is that they range from the very early grade right up into graduate education. I remember a Professor Joseph Smith who taught a graduate seminar in literature. He used to read Shakespeare aloud in class, and, as I listened to the language and also the evocative power of his voice, I was struck that it was his method that really taught me that literature is not an ancient study. It is an inquiry into the deepest yearnings of the human spirit.

I remember Mr Whittlinger, a high school teacher, who stopped me after class one day and said: 'Ernest, you are doing very well in History. You keep this up and you just might be a student.' That was the highest academic accolade I had ever had, but he hit me at the right time – a little kid who was not sure whether I was a cowboy or a base-ball player. Mr Whittlinger gave me an option that had not really occurred to me. He had me think about an academic interest that had perhaps been there latently, but never stirred.

I even remember my first grade teacher. On my way to school in Dayton, Ohio, I was walking with my mother and I asked if I would learn to read that day. My mother and father had this irritating habit of writing notes to one another, and my brothers and I were not 'in the loop' – as they say in Washington. So, I wanted to go to school to master the adult code. My mother said: 'No. You wont learn to read today, but you will before the year is out'. Well, she did not tell me about Miss Rice! I walked into the room and there she stood. She looked at twenty-eight frightened, awe-struck children, and said: 'Good morning, class today we learn to read'. Those were the first words I ever heard in school. We spent all day on four words: 'I go to school'. We traced them, we sang them, and we even prayed them. I thought of Miss Rice several years ago when I wrote a book called *College*, because I had a chapter right up front, entitled *The Centrality of Language*. It occurred to me that it was a first-grade teacher, who established very early in my life that language is the centre-piece of learning, that it is not just another subject but the means by which all subjects are pursued.

I mention these examples as a reminder that teaching is the process by which the continuity of scholarship is sustained, and that there is absolutely no way to maintain it except through transmission across the generations. I find it really disquieting that in the academy today good teaching is not adequately rewarded. In the US, you are given research 'opportunities'. But, then you are also given a teaching 'load'. The teaching assignment is a load. Research is an opportunity. But after you have been given your teaching load you are penalised if you spend too much time with students. It is 'catch twenty-two', especially for the young professoriate who have not yet achieved status and full-time tenure. In the US, it is much better for a professor to deliver a paper at the Hyatt Hotel in Chicago, than it is to teach undergraduates back home. Robert Oppenheimer in a lecture at the two-hundredth anniversary of Columbia University spoke eloquently of the professor as mentor, and he placed teaching at the very heart of the scholarly endeavour. Oppenheimer said:

> It is the proper role of the scientist that he not merely discover a new truth, but also that he teach, that he try to bring the most honest and the most intelligent account of new knowledge to all who will try to learn.

Surely this means teaching future scholars in the classroom?

What does all this have to do with the next century? I am convinced that universities must deepen their commitment to the scholarship of teaching. The diversity of students now coming into the nation's classrooms is very great. If we do not seriously attend to the pedagogical obligations that are involved we will fail, both educationally and ethically, to fulfil our mission.

Good teaching also means engaging the new technology to enrich instruction and to extend learning beyond the campus. Above all, it means adjusting the calendar and the clock, trying to serve the needs of part-time students and adults, since in the century ahead learning will surely be life-long. During my days as Chancellor in New York, in the late 'sixties and early 'seventies – when I was being pushed around and shouted down and locked out by students – a group of young students came to me one day and said: 'Why do you have us sit in a class all day? There are other ways to learn. Why is there not an institution here that is more flexible, that allows for independent study?' And, I thought: 'They are absolutely right. Not all students need to line up for fifty minutes, three times a week'. So we created something called the Empire State College in New York within the SUNY system. It was a non-campus college, in which students could study independently. Well, that college has, in fact, thrived and, twenty years later, has established a great example in our country of non-traditional study. The only little foot-note is that the students who wanted that college did not attend. The ones who did come were twenty-five, and thirty- and forty- and fifty-year-old adults who found it convenient to study independently with mentors and with contracts, and to organise learning around their own schedules, not the convenience of the institution. I am suggesting that a reaffirmation of teaching will be essential if the lifelong interests of the students of the coming century are to be met – especially those from the new minorities, part-timers, and those finding their way with the help of technology and special scheduling of classes.

Conclusion

Scholarship, then, means the discovery of new knowledge through research, but that is only the beginning. To avoid pedantry scholarship must also integrate knowledge. To avoid irrelevance, knowledge must be applied. And, to avoid discontinuity, knowledge must be transmitted to future generations through great teaching. And all of these are inter-dependent, and interact dynamically. The past has allowed us to focus on the scholarship of discovery. But, increasingly, in the next century we will have to integrate that knowledge, apply it, and communicate it through teaching to each new generation. And so universities will have reinterpret their role. It would be fool-hardy and ultimately destructive not to hold fast to the traditions of integrity and independence that have made the university one of human-kind's most enduring institutions. But even the best of institutions must evolve and for the university of the twenty-first century this means giving the honourable term scholarship a broader, more capacious, meaning – one that brings legitimacy to the full range of academic work. What is needed is a network of diverse and responsive institutions, with each university taking pride in its own distinctive mission, seeking to complement rather than imitate the others. Looking to the next century I am convinced that such networks will, increasingly, become global as scholars all around the world are collaborating, engaging in research, looking for connections, searching for solutions to vexing social problems, and communicating their knowledge effectively to students. What I envision, then, is an international community of learning – one in which scholarship, broadly defined, will lead not only to the renewal of the university, but ultimately to the renewal of society itself, and to the building of a better world.

Discussion

Barry Seward-Thompson (Consultant, Open Minds): Everything that you have talked about can be applied to scholarship as it is looked at today – as based very largely on knowledge. But as we move forward in the next century, releasing people's full potential is going to be of great importance, and self-knowledge and self-awareness seem to me a major part of that. The phrase *scholarship of self-awareness* does not sound quite right, but I feel there is a real danger one could achieve everything you have been talking about – the four scholarships – without really getting at the potential that is hidden in the 90% of the brain which is the unconscious.

Dr Boyer: It is fair to summarise my position on scholarship by saying it is knowledge-based. This is the familiar and, perhaps, the primary territory of the academic community. I respect profoundly the idea that there is a great part of us that goes beyond cerebration and the cognitive and I think I can make a connection with what you say and my last category – through great teaching. That is where you are talking about the whole person. The outstanding teachers I encountered had four characteristics in common. First of all, they were well informed – there was knowledge there. Second, they had the capacity to relate what they knew to the reality of student experience. They connected at a point of familiarity and then moved beyond. Third, they created a kind of active learning in the classroom – there was give and take, and students became sufficiently empowered that occasionally the teacher, in turn, became a student. But finally – and this gets to the point you made – the great teachers I had were authentic human beings. There was something about who they were that appealed to me beyond their knowledge and even beyond even their pedagogical capacity. They were three-dimensional. They were willing to say when they did not know the answer. They became vulnerable. But they were whole individuals, integrated, willing to give themselves and not just knowledge. In the *scholarship of teaching*, I would argue, a sense of wholeness begins to develop which brings the whole brain together.

Dr John Daniel (Vice-Chancellor, Open University): I am very much taken with your concept of the *scholarship of integration*. At the Open University, when we do courses which take a multi-disciplinary approach – on the Enlightenment, for example, or a Third World topic – they are enormously popular with students. Obviously, if we are to value this particular aspect of scholarship in the more conventional setting, there has to be some way in which the professoriate can demonstrate it to their colleagues. The two obvious outlets seem to have problems. In conventional classroom teaching – at least as I experienced it in North America – the teacher who is too original and who brings too many things into the course is, in fact, rather tiresome for the colleagues who are teaching around that course. In the same way, we are already complaining that even the output of hard, succinct research is clogging up the worlds' libraries with journals. Probably, by definition, the scholarship of integration requires a more discursive and free-wheeling kind of outlet. Have you any suggestions as to how we who are managing universities might try to evaluate such scholarship?

Dr Boyer: In the US, we are in the process of developing national standards of testing. It is going to be a vicious battle because we have a local system that has suddenly gone national. We have a national goal which says we should test students in all the basic subjects at the twelfth, eighth and fourth grade levels. The basic subjects are to be defined in very rigid categories called Carnegie units – a term our Foundation invented, unhappily, sixty years ago. But these are very rigid categories of knowledge which we call disciplines and, of course, you cannot define a discipline any more. Nevertheless, we are going to tell fourth-graders that there are disciplines and they had better prepare to think within those boxes. I am worried about that – and not just in relation to the universities – because the more you go down into the early grades, the less children think in boxes. They think much more broadly. I am worried that those categories are going to shape the way we frame the curriculum in the schools for the next century. I am not hostile to the disciplines. They have served us very well. I want to stress that. On the other hand, they do not form a sufficient territory for intellectual inquiry. And yet, if you venture too far beyond them, there is no reward, and you are looked at with some suspicion.

The challenge is to bridge the disciplines comfortably and not carelessly. For example, I think universities can begin to create the right climate by hosting public forums on inter-disciplinary issues, in which faculty members from different fields can engage in public discourse. Students will then begin to see that these disciplinary arrangements have a root – which is important – but that there are connections across the disciplines as well. This can be modelled in the first instance informally, in seminars, and then demonstrated to the larger community. I know that some of the faculty members in our general education programme in the United States are organising around cross-disciplinary seminars for the freshman and sophomore levels. There is a big discussion whether general education – which I know is a peculiarly American approach to the first two years of college – might be organised more thematically, rather than just getting those units 'out of the way' before moving on to a speciality.

So the task now is to create courses organised around a theme – important social issues, for example, or great ideas. That would force the academics to join in because no single one would have sufficient skill and insight to handle such a course alone. While I think that the formal structure of the university will continue, for many years yet, to be discipline-based, something is happening at the outer edges where the old typology is not working very well. The most interesting research institutes and organisations are being built around inter-disciplinary questions. I would predict that by the year 2050 we are going to have a totally new typology of knowledge. The change will be as dramatic as occurred in the nineteenth century when the sciences toppled philosophy. In the twenty-first century we will not recognise the current categories.

The reasons are two-fold. One is the internal imperative, from the disciplines themselves, as key questions are formulated which do not fit the old boxes. But, secondly, there is going to be tremendous pressure from external imperatives. The survival questions – health, the environment and economic issues – are going to be so acute, well into the twenty-first century, that universities will rearrange the questions that they are studying and the research projects they are designing, in order to respond to them. The internal imperatives and intellectual questions among scholars will need inter-disciplinary formulations. And the external imperatives of human survival will demand the restructuring of the research questions and also the kind of intellectual questions that are discussed within the curriculum itself. It is a matter of transition. Within fifty years or so I think we will see a re-design of what we call the disciplines that will be far more inter-disciplinary in structure.

Professor Brian Gomes da Costa (Director, Bath College of Higher Education): For an administrator, the practical problem is to reward teaching. There is quite a distinction between the scholarship of discovery, integration and application on the one hand and teaching on the other. The first three are institutionalised and independent of the individual. There are international journals, international conferences and communication which are not individual-dependent. The scholarship of teaching seems to be, essentially, a local matter and there does not seem to be an analogue – an 'institutionalisation' of teaching – so that it can be grasped by other minds and criticised in the same way that discovery, integration and application, all of which usually come to be published, can be criticised. I have great difficulty in seeing how teaching can be rewarded in the absence of the analogue to the first three.

Dr Boyer: It will, indeed, be necessary to figure out a reward system with some degree of credibility so that quality is maintained. The reason research and publication are so prominent is not because academics want to run from students. There is no conspiracy here. A nomenclature and a credibility has been developed which is accepted across the campus, and has currency within the academy, nationally and internationally. We know how to evaluate refereed journals. To talk about other dimensions of assessment, without having thoughtfully developed credible evaluative arrangements, will leave them vulnerable and never fully embraced, because to be rewarded is, in fact, to affirm the importance of the additional function. In the end, I think you can make judgements about skill in integration. At the very highest level, the writings of Stephen J Gould and Lewis Thomas, in our country, and Stephen Hawkings's memorable essay, *The History of Time*, are examples of integration. I think you can have peer review there. Peer review does not have to be only about the footnotes to the footnotes. You can get people who can bring solid judgements as to whether this is serious integrated work or simply a kind of grooving in the grass. As far as application is concerned, we have not worked at this recently in the United States but I think we can develop standards that deal with the application of knowledge and even ask for judgements from those who have been served. The sources of information matter.

Teaching, on the other hand, has become perhaps the liveliest topic among US administrators and some faculty in the last few years, and the pressure to think further about criteria of evaluation is great. At our Foundation, we are beginning to work on another report, tentatively titled *Scholarship Assessed*. Faculty in the US and Britain want credibility which goes beyond the applause of the student in the classroom, but until there is agreement about the standards to be established nothing can be done. We are just beginning. I am still optimistic, and there is a lot of interest among the professional associations in the United States that we might at least improve the criteria for evaluating teaching and get some language and agreements that might provide a familiar grid that could be used in résumés. There are only three sources of information: peer evaluation, personal evaluation and student evaluation. I think all three can be used. In personal evaluation you can put on paper the processes you used as a teacher, and others can evaluate that to see whether you had goals and how you went at it. It does not mean you are a great teacher, but at least it indicates there is an intellectual exercise at work. Peer evaluation takes place through observation and interview. I believe in student evaluation, with one caveat. I think students should never be asked to evaluate a teacher unless they have had a seminar in how to do so. Just to throw a sheet in front of them and tell them to fill in the check marks – they will deal with that as trivially as such a process suggests. At the beginning of the year, students should be advised that one of their tasks will be to assess faculty members. This is not widely done in the US. Every year I was evaluated by the students at Princeton and this went right to the Dean's office. It was routine in the system. However time must be taken to talk about the process, to state the criteria and to tell the students it must be taken as seriously as they want the faculty to take their evaluation. That would be to create an understanding of the process which greatly increased its validity.

I know the sources of the information, but exactly what the criteria might be is still to be fully developed. The hope for some inter-campus understanding might be wildly optimistic but, until it is achieved, faculty will be sceptical about devoting much time to something which will not build to a larger credit within the profession. Some of the ranking universities in the US are insisting, in their interviews of staff, that they provide documentation of good teaching. The idea that teaching is an important part of the professional life is beginning to build. But, lest I be misunderstood, I do not mean that you can be a great teacher and not have an absolutely solid research base. That would be foolish. But at least teaching is being jockeyed into a position of being judged of greater merit than it was in recent years.

The University of California has just revised its personnel policies to allow for a super grade in teaching – there has been a super grade in research for many years. This suggests that teaching distinction can put you in a super grade of salary as well as institutional prestige – still assuming however, that you are well recognised in your discipline. It is allowing a little more equity in terms of the importance of teaching in university life.

Peter Mathias (Master, Downing College, Cambridge): You place great emphasis on the relationship between teaching and research and the importance, institutionally, of the linkages and inter-relationships. There are, however, very powerful trends whereby research, particularly in some of the most exciting and most rapidly advancing fields such as medicine or physics, is leaving the universities altogether, for national and international research institutes. Furthermore, in this country a new mode of funding has been established for research, which is now separately assessed from teaching. This may, in the future, drive research from its connections and its single matrix with teaching. I wondered if you could say how you see such trends in the US and how you see the future in that respect.

Dr Boyer: The same trends exist in the US and are accelerating. Federal funding for research has been the primary source since the end of World War II. Before that there had been no research funds to speak of. After the war two great events converged: a new generation of scholars came down from the research centres and tried to clone that experience, and there was the Federal cornucopia which enabled research – which had been viewed as for the few – to become an option for the many. That, in effect, created a research culture and established the notion of peace-time research as being channelled through the universities. For fifty years, we have assumed that the universities are the primary base of research, that research is a renewing dimension intellectually and that it also has a great capacity to spill over into graduate and undergraduate teaching. The two are now being uncoupled. There is a frustration among Federal funders that universities have been careless in the use of their research monies, diverting them to auxiliary functions. There is a big debate on how much money is needed to support research. Funding is slowing down and universities are scrambling for alternatives, in industry and business especially. Free-standing institutes are being created. Even the institutes which have received Federal funds have become increasingly disengaged. They can be part of the university organisation but operate as a total island of intellectual distance. I worry very much, at least in our culture, about research being increasingly disengaged from university life. But that is the trend. Independent contracts are being entered into with corporations which tend, very early on, to divert loyalties and even basic findings into a profit-making structure.

Dr Jack Hobbs (Assistant Principal, Sheffield Hallam University): You have made no comment about the growth of knowledge outside the university sector – particularly with the development of knowledge-based industries which are likely to increase rapidly over the next few years – and to the extent to which the total student experience might benefit from a partnership with agencies outside the university sector. Secondly – and this refers to the scholarship of application – it seems that, at present, the British Government looks on the professional activity of staff in the application area as being the responsibility of industrial or other organisations, rather than that of Government. Yet if the Government is not involved in the funding models, and the accolades lie elsewhere, a situation could result in which short-termism might prevail in the partnership with external organisations. If that were the case, the application model would quickly recede as a potential model for the future.

Dr Boyer: We have historically, and perhaps even sentimentally, assumed that universities are the well-spring of knowledge. I think those days have passed, if they ever did exist. In this series of lectures, Hans van Ginkel has made the point that information is spreading so rapidly to other sectors and is being generated so actively that the universities may, in the end, become the integrators. This is an interesting point. But to pretend that we do not have great centres of knowledge outside the university, especially in industry and business, would be foolish. In fact, the universities are finding the greatest competitors are industry research centres. General Electric and Bell Laboratories hire as many PhDs as the largest US universities – and at pretty good pay.

I do not know what the nature of the partnership will be in the days ahead. I am troubled if contracts become so cosy that the university becomes an extension of any single corporate research effort. That is not an anti-industry statement: it is a question of the different missions of these institutions. The ideal would be – and I know of no example in the US where this functions well – to have periodic seminars in which the autonomy and purposes of the two institutions are maintained, but where they can collaborate around new directions. The contract would not specify a predetermined product, but some of the best minds in the country would be involved in thinking about and redesigning models for the future. I can envisage that kind of curiosity-driven, collaborative, effort rather than the narrower contracts which are occurring now. I think it would be remiss if we did not try modelling new kinds of partnership that would not invade the integrity of the university but would demonstrate collaboration in the intellectual world.

The Government might help with this. In the US, for example, the National Science Foundation is creating interdisciplinary seminars built around university scholars, but I can see no reason why industry scholars should not be invited. However, I have observed that some industries are uncomfortable about talking too freely in those settings because they might give away trade secrets.

Professor Noel Entwistle (University of Edinburgh): You seem to be quite optimistic about the way forward for the four forms of scholarship. But one could, on the basis of the same evidence, be profoundly pessimistic. You cite the importance of research and say at the same time that perhaps fewer than one hundred of the several thousand universities in the States would be able to have that at the core of their activities. Subsequently, we have talked about the research institutes outside the universities that are taking over those functions. So the role of research within universities overall may be decreasing. You say that research should be integrated and you gave examples of where this is happening: but the examples you gave were actually of integration very narrowly focused on research problems. You say we need to have a scholarship of application. In this country research money is increasingly for policy-oriented research, to the extent that fundamental research is being squeezed out altogether in some areas. We say we should have quality in teaching, and yet the first pressure that came on university staff was to improve their research output, and departments were judged on that. Now, belatedly there is equivalent pressure to improve the quality of teaching. Are we going to expect all our staff to do all these things? If so, nervous breakdowns are going to be even more common than they already are.

Dr Boyer: You could build a strong case that the trends are all in one direction, and an equally strong case that they are all in the other. I would weigh in on the side of integration. The big and interesting areas seem to be moving towards reconfiguration. The big social questions which are emerging rapidly are by nature integrative. The Aids crisis, for example, generated huge amounts of money overnight, and even reorganised the curriculum in the schools around a social imperative that was so very ominous and disturbing. Part of the research effort is very specialised, but the social implications are very broad.

In regard to teaching, I have been really impressed over the past two to three years by the number of universities in America that are really enquiring into the value and importance of teaching undergraduates. For the first time in fifty years the issue of how to strike a better balance in the role of the faculty is very much a topic which is alive and well, and it has just grown exponentially. But the jury is still out on whether faculty will be rewarded if they weight their own professional lives more towards teaching than regular publication. One of the reasons why I began tonight by discussing the history of the university is to remind us how short-lived the current model is. The only thing that is unchanging is change. The current more limited culture of what universities should be doing and how faculty should be rewarded is only thirty years old, or less. The university is not going to remain static, and my sense is that it is changing towards a more fluid model.